D1570747

HYPOGLYCEMIA CONTROL COOKERY

by Dorothy Tompkins Revell,
Registered Dietitian, R.D., ADA

BERKLEY BOOKS, NEW YORK

This Berkley book contains the complete
text of the original hardcover edition.
It has been completely reset in a typeface
designed for easy reading, and was printed
from new film.

HYPOGLYCEMIA CONTROL COOKERY

A Berkley Book / published by arrangement with
Royal Publications, Inc.

PRINTING HISTORY
Royal Publications edition published 1973
Berkley edition / November 1973
Thirteenth printing / September 1983

ISBN: 0-425-05734-8

A BERKLEY BOOK ® TM 757,375
Berkley Books are published by The Berkley Publishing Group,
200 Madison Avenue, New York, New York 10016.
The name "BERKLEY" and the stylized "B" with design
are trademarks belonging to Berkley Publishing Corporation.
PRINTED IN THE UNITED STATES OF AMERICA

CONTENTS

Introduction:

Hypoglycemia Diet

Spontaneous hypoglycemia or low blood sugar represents a disorder in carbohydrate metabolism. An over-production of insulin or hyperinsulinism is the direct cause. Symptoms are weakness, trembling, sweating, extreme hunger, and, in severe cases, convulsions and unconsciousness.

When the pancreas is over-stimulated the result is an increase in the production of insulin. If the meal is high in quickly digested and absorbed carbohydrates, the carbohydrates will serve as the stimulus to this situation.

The dietary treatment is to prevent a marked rise in the blood sugar. The diet will be one high in protein foods. Protein foods are meats, fish, poultry, cheese, eggs, and milk. Because of the carbohydrate milk sugar, lactose, the amount of milk in the diet will be limited. The carbohydrate content for the day will be limited from 75 to 100 grams, with a further reduction to 50 grams if the individual does not show improvement. There will be an avoidance or restriction on the concentrated sweets as candy, sugar, jellies, jams, marmalades, honey, syrups, molasses, etc. Butter, margarine, mayonnaise, cream salad dressings, bacon, nuts, oils, and other fat foods will meet the caloric requirement for individuals. It is best to have the food for the day spread out with three meals and interval feedings during midmorning, midafternoon, and evening snacks. *The spacing of the food is very important.* It is suggested that the carbohydrate for the day be divided as evenly as possible with protein and fat to supply the body with a continuous flow of glucose. If 75 grams of carbohydrate are allowed for the day, then 25 grams or thereabouts, for each of the three meals is an example of distribution. Sometimes it is necessary to carry cheese and crackers to control frequent attacks.

Stress must be given to follow your physician's instructions. These recipes may be used in your menu planning for the day. It will be necessary to recognize the grams of carbohydrate per serving in the daily allowance. With a prudent approach to the meal pattern you will be able to have a well balanced nutritional diet.

Special suggestions in addition to those already mentioned include:

1. The carbohydrate in the diet is restricted and that allowed will come from the indicated amount of the bread, crackers, cereal, potato, rice, corn, noodles, macaroni, spaghetti, lima beans, baked beans, milk, fruit, beets, peas, onions, pumpkin, carrots, turnips, squash, rutabaga, calculated extra food items and recipes.
2. The protein in the diet is not restricted. Have generous servings.
3. The fat in the diet is not restricted or modified unless so indicated by the physician's order.
4. Salt, pepper, herbs, relishes are not restricted, unless so ordered by the physician.

5. Fruits will be fresh, dried, water packed, or with artificial sweeteners but not with sugar or syrup.
6. Vegetables not indicated in (1) may be used liberally.
7. Artificial sweeteners and Dzerta gelatin may be used.
8. Coffee has a high content of caffeine and caffeine will stimulate the pancreas to release more insulin, for this reason limit the intake of coffee or avoid the usage. Tea is also high in caffeine but since it is more apt to be drunk weak than strong, does not need to be restricted. Sanka does not contain as high a percentage of caffeine and may be used as desired.

Suggested Menus

	Carbohydrate Grams
Breakfast	
½ cup orange juice	10
1 slice of toast	15
butter or margarine	
2 slices of cheese	
coffee	
Noon-Luncheon	
roast turkey with gravy	
½ cup mashed potatoes	15
buttered broccoli	
tossed salad with oil/vinegar salad dressing	
cranberry relish	
butter or margarine	
tea	

Dinner	*Carbohydrate Grams*
cold sliced turkey	
cottage cheese with chives	
lettuce wedge with sliced tomatoes and salad dressing	
1 slice of bread, white or dark	15
butter or margarine	
1 small baked apple with cream	10
tea	

Feedings (midmorning, midafternoon, evening)

5 saltine crackers, can be divided among the 3 feedings	15
sliced turkey/sliced cheese	
total carbohydrate	80 grams

Breakfast

½ grapefruit section	10
scrambled egg with parsley	
1 slice of toast	15
butter or margarine	
sliced ham	
coffee	

Noon-Luncheon

broth soup	
turkey salad on lettuce leaves	
1 dinner roll	15
butter or margarine	
sliced tomatoes and cucumbers and seasonings desired	
1 cup milk	12

Dinner

roast beef with horseradish relish	
1 small baked potato	15
buttered asparagus	
green goddess salad	
½ peach, sliced, cream if desired	10
tea	

Feedings   (midmorning, midafternoon, evening)

1 slice of bread, divided among the 3 feedings	15
sliced roast beef/cheese	
total carbohydrate	92 grams

Breakfast	*Carbohydrate Grams*

½ cup fruit cocktail — 10
2 small pancakes with low calorie syrup — 15
4–6 small link sausages
coffee

Noon-Luncheon

French onion soup
chef's salad with salad dressing
4 saltine crackers — 12
1 cup milk — 12
coffee if desired

Dinner

1 serving of beef casserole dinner — 15
spinach with lemon juice
sliced tomatoes and radish roses
cole slaw salad
½ a small banana, sliced with cream — 10
tea

Feedings   (midmorning, midafternoon, evening)

2 graham crackers, can be divided among the 3
   feedings — 15
cheese/cold meat

total carbohydrate	89 grams

Breakfast

V-8 cocktail juice
¾ cup cornflake cereal — 15
½ cup milk — 6
1 slice of toast — 15
butter or margarine
sanka or coffee

Noon-Luncheon

fruit salad on lettuce leaves with 24-hour salad
   dressing — 10
cottage cheese
½ slice of bread — 7
butter or margarine
pecan nut meats
tea

Dinner   *Carbohydrate Grams*

leg of lamb with mint sauce
1 small baked potato   15
buttered Brussel sprouts
shredded lettuce with salad dressing
½ fresh pear   5
tea

Feedings (midmorning, midafternoon, evening)

5 saltine crackers, divided among the 3 feedings   15
cheese spread/cold meat/peanuts
                                        _____
              total carbohydrate   88 grams

Breakfast

1 small orange, sliced   10
1 soft-boiled egg
3 slices Canadian bacon
1 slice toast   15
butter or margarine
sanka

Noon-Luncheon

tomato juice
hamburger patty on ½ hamburger bun   15
catsup, pickle relish
tossed salad with salad dressing
tea

Dinner

oven-baked chicken
buttered winter squash (½ cup)   7
1 small baked potato   15
lettuce/cucumber/tomato salad with dressing
⅔ cup strawberry Bavarian dessert   5
tea

Feedings (midmorning, midafternoon, evening)

8 round Ritz crackers, can be divided
    among the 3 feedings   15
cheese spread/sliced cheese/cold meat
                                        _____
              total carbohydrate   82 grams

Breakfast   *Carbohydrate Grams*

½ grapefruit	10
½ English muffin, toasted	15
1 poached egg served on the muffin half	
4 slices of crisp bacon	
coffee	

Noon-Luncheon

tuna fish salad served on lettuce leaves	
stuffed celery stalks with soft cheese spread	
1 small dinner roll	15
butter or margarine	
tea	

Dinner

steak with mushrooms	
1 small baked potato	15
buttered string beans	
fruit salad with 24-hour salad dressing	10
relish for steak if desired	
coffee	

Feedings (midmorning, midafternoon, evening)

20 oyster crackers, can be divided among the 3 feedings	15
cheese/sardines/cold meat	
total carbohydrate	80 grams

Breakfast

½ cup orange juice	10
½ cup cooked oatmeal	15
½ cup milk	6
1 slice toast	15
butter or margarine	
artificial sweetener for cereal if desired	

Noon-Luncheon

tomato consommé soup	
broiled cheese on 1 slice of toast	15
sliced ham	
cole slaw	
dill pickles	
tea	

Dinner   *Carbohydrate Grams*

salmon steak with sliced lemon
1 small boiled potato   15
½ cup buttered carrots and small onions   7
green goddess salad
coffee

Feedings (midmorning, midafternoon, evening)

3 Ry-Krisp, can be divided among the 3 feedings   15
butter or margarine
small amount of peanut butter allowed on
   each Ry-Krisp
cheese slices

                        total carbohydrate   98 grams

Carbohydrate Content of Some Common Food

Carbohydrate Content Does Not Need to Be Considered

Asparagus	Greens:	Lettuce
Beans, string	beets	Mushrooms
Broccoli	chard	Okra
Brussels sprouts	collard	Peppers
Cabbage	dandelion	Pimiento
Cauliflower	kale	Radish
Celery	kohlrabi	Sauerkraut
Chicory	mustard	Summer squash
Cucumber	spinach	Tomatoes and juice
Eggplant	turnip	
Escarole		

Carbohydrate Content for ½ Cup, Cooked or Raw, Is 7 Grams

Beets	Pumpkin
Carrots	Rutabagas
Onions	Squash, winter
Peas	Turnips

Carbohydrate Content for the Following Is 12 Grams

Milk, whole	1 cup
Milk, 2%	1 cup
Milk, skim	1 cup
Milk, buttermilk	1 cup
Milk, powdered, whole	¼ cup
Milk, powdered, skim	¼ cup
Yoghurt, made from skim milk	1 cup
Yoghurt, made from whole milk	1 cup
Cream Soup	1 cup
Eggnog, no sweetener added	1 cup

Carbohydrate Content of the Following Is 10 Grams

Fruits (may be fresh, dried, cooked, canned or frozen
  without sugar)

Apple (2″ diameter)	1 small
Applesauce	½ cup
Apricots	2 medium
Apricots, dried	4 halves
Avocado, pitted	½ medium
Banana	½ small
Blackberries, boysenberries, raspberries, straw-berries (fresh, frozen, or canned)	1 cup
Blueberries, gooseberries (fresh, frozen or canned)	⅔ cup
Cantaloupe (6″ diameter)	¼ melon
Cherries, fresh	10 large
Cherries, Maraschino	4
Dates	2
Figs, fresh	2 large
Fruit Cocktail	½ cup
Grapefruit	½ small
Grapes, green or red	12 large
Honeydew melon	¼ melon
Kumquats	4 medium
Mango	1 small
Nectarine	1 medium
Orange	1 small
Papaya (½ cup or cubes)	⅓ small
Peach	1 medium
Pear	1 small
Persimmons	½ medium
Pineapple	½ cup
Pineapple ring, large	1½ rings
Plums (2″ diameter)	2 medium
Pomegranate	½ medium
Prunes, dried	2 medium
Pumpkin, canned	½ cup
Raisins	2 tablespoons
Tangerine	1 large
Watermelon, balls, cubes	1 cup
(10″ x ¾″ thick)	½ slice

Juices

Apple juice	⅓ cup	Lime juice	½ cup
Apricot juice	⅓ cup	Orange juice	½ cup
Grape juice	¼ cup	Pineapple juice	⅓ cup
Grapefruit juice	½ cup	Prune juice	¼ cup
Lemon juice	½ cup		

Carbohydrate Content of the Following Is 15 Grams

Beans & peas (lima, navy, cowpeas, etc.)	½ cup cooked
Corn	⅓ cup
Corn	½ small cob
Parsnips	⅓ cup
Potatoes:	
white	1 small
baked (2″ diameter)	1
mashed, boiled	½ cup
hashed brown	½ cup
Potato substitutes (rice, noodles, macaroni, spaghetti, grits)	½ cup cooked
Potato, sweet or yam	¼ cup
Potato chips	1 cup
Potato chips	15 or 1 ounce bag
Potato sticks, shoestring potatoes	⅔ cup
Potatoes, French fried	10 (2″ long pieces)
Wild rice	3 tablespoons

Miscellaneous Foods Showing the Carbohydrate Value

Food	Amount	Grams Carbohydrate
Butterscotch balls	2	10
Caramel, plain	1 medium	10
Chocolate, baking, bitter	1 ounce or 1 square	10
Chocolate syrup	1 tablespoon, level	20
Fondant patties or mints	1 average (40/pound)	10
Gum drops	1 large	10
Gum drops	10 small	10
Hershey Kisses, milk chocolate	5	10
Honey	2 teaspoons	10
Jam or jelly, commercial	2 teaspoons	10
Jelly beans	7	10
Lemon drops	5	10
Life Savers	6	10
Malted milk, powder	1 tablespoon, level	10
Marshmallows, large	2	10
Molasses	2 teaspoons	10
Popsicle	½ of twin bar	10
Sugar:		
brown	2 teaspoons	10
white, granulated	2½ teaspoons	10
Powdered	1 tablespoon	10

| Syrup, corn | 2 teaspoons | 10 |
| Sugar, cubed | 5 small | 10 |

Carbohydrate Content of the Following Is 15 Grams

Animal crackers	10
Arrowroot cookies	4
Bagel	½
Banana bread (3½" x 3½" x ⅜")	1 slice
Boston brown bread (3" diameter x ½")	1 slice
Bread crumbs, dry	3 tablespoons
Bread, plain, light, or dark	1 slice
Bread, raisin (uniced)	1 slice
Bread stuffing	¼ cup
Bread sticks (3½" long)	2
Cereal, cooked	½ cup
Cereal, dry—see listing of various brands on pages 25–26	
Cheese Nips	30
Chinese noodles	½ cup
Cream Puff (shell only)	1 small
Corn stick (5" long)	1 average
Crackers:	
graham	2
oyster (about 20)	½ cup
saltines (2" squares)	5
soda (2½" squares)	3
round (1½" diameter)	8
Doughnut, plain or raised	1
English Muffin	½
Flour	2 tablespoons
French, Italian, Vienna Bread (½" thick)	1 slice
French toast	1 slice
Fritos	¼ cup
Gingerale	¾ cup
Ginger snaps	5
Grapenuts	¼ cup
Holland Rusks	1½ biscuits
Ice cream	½ cup
Ice milk	½ cup
JellO, regular, any flavor	½ cup
JELLO, regular, any flavor	½ cup
Lady Fingers	3 large or 6 small
Korn Kurls	1 ounce bag
Lasagna	½ cup
Jerusalem artichokes (1½" diameter, raw)	4 small
Macaroons	1 large

Malted milk (plain, dry)	2 tablespoons
Melba toast	4 pieces
Marshmallows	3 average
Matzo square	¾
Matzo round	1
Matzo meal	3 tablespoons
Muffin	1
Oatmeal cookies (3" diameter)	1 medium
Pancake (4" diameter)	1 average
Pizza (3" x 4")	1 piece
Plain sugar cookies (4" diameter)	1
Popover	1 average
Popcorn (unbuttered)	1½ cups
Pretzels	5 medium twists or 1 Dutch pretzel
Pretzels, very thin	60
Roll, hard (2" diameter)	½
Roll, Parkerhouse	1
Ry-Krisp	3
Shredded wheat biscuit	½ large
Salsify or vegetable oyster plant	⅔ cup
Sherbet	¼ cup
Tomato sauce	½ cup
Tortilla, Mexican (6" diameter)	3
Vanilla wafer	6
Waffle (frozen)	1 small
Wheat germ	3 tablespoons
Zwieback	3

Carbohydrate Content 22 Grams

Custard	½ cup
Cornstarch vanilla pudding	½ cup
Dairy Queen	½ cup
Fruit cake (3" x 2¾" x ½")	1 piece
Pie crust	⅛ of a single 9" shell
Waffle	5½" diameter

Carbohydrate Content 30 Grams

Bun:	
frankfurter	1
hamburger	1
Bun, raisin	1 average

Carbohydrate Content 40 Grams

Coca-Cola, Seven-Up, Pepsi-Cola	12 ounces
Gingerale	16 ounces

Information As Supplied by the Manufacturer of Commercial Products

Soup

Brand	Food	Serving According to Directions	Carbohydrate Grams
Campbell Soup	Tomato	1 cup	15
	Tomato, Bisque of	1 cup	7
	Tomato Rice, Old Fashioned	1 cup	7
	Asparagus, Cream of	1 cup	7
	Clam Chowder (Manhattan Style)	1 cup	7
	Golden Vegetable Noodle-O's	1 cup	7
	Minestrone	1 cup	7
	Celery, Cream of	1 cup	7
	Chicken, Cream of	1 cup	7
	Golden Mushroom	1 cup	7
	Oyster	1 cup	7
	Mushroom, Cream of	1 cup	7
	Chicken Vegetable	1 cup	7
	Noodles and Ground Beef	1 cup	7
	Pepper Pot	1 cup	7
	Scotch Broth	1 cup	7
	Turkey Noodle	1 cup	7
	Turkey Vegetable	1 cup	7

Frozen Vegetable with Beef, Old Fashioned	1 cup	7
Black Bean	1 cup	15
Tomato-Beef Noodle-O's	1 cup	15
Frozen Green Pea with Ham	1 cup	15
Bean with Bacon	1 cup	22
Chili Beef	1 cup	22
Green Pea	1 cup	22
Beef	1 cup	7
Hot Dog Bean	1 cup	22
Split Pea with Ham	1 cup	22
Chicken Gumbo	1 cup	7
Chicken Noodle	1 cup	7
Chicken Noodle-O's	1 cup	7
Chicken with Rice	1 cup	7
Chicken with Stars	1 cup	7
Onion	1 cup	4
Vegetable and Beef Stockpot	1 cup	7
Vegetable Beef	1 cup	7
Vegetable	1 cup	15
Vegetarian Vegetable	1 cup	15

Soup

Brand	Food	Serving According to Directions	Carbohydrate Grams
	Vegetable, Old Fashioned	1 cup	7
	Cheddar Cheese	1 cup	7
	Frozen Clam Chowder (New England Style)	1 cup	7
	Frozen Oyster Stew	1 cup	7
	Frozen Shrimp, Cream of	1 cup	7
	Chicken 'n Dumplings	1 cup	4
	Potato, Cream of	1 cup	10
Heinz Company	Bean with Smoked Pork	1 cup	22
	Beef Noodle	1 cup	7
	Celery, Cream of	1 cup	7
	Chicken and Star Noodles	1 cup	10
	Chicken, Cream of	1 cup	7
	Chicken Noodle	1 cup	7
	Chicken Vegetable	1 cup	7
	Chicken with Rice	1 cup	22
	Chili with Beef	1 cup	22
	Mushroom, Cream of	1 cup	10
	Split Pea with Ham	1 cup	15
	Tomato	1 cup	15

Turkey Noodle	1 cup	10
Vegetable Beef	1 cup	7
Vegetable Beef Stock	1 cup	12
Vegetarian Vegetable (without meat)	1 cup	15
Heinz Great American Soup Do Not Dilute		
Abundant Vegetarian Vegetable	1 cup	18
Bountiful Chicken Noodle with Dumplings	1 cup	10
Buttered Tomato with Vegetables	1 cup	15
Delicious Beef Noodle with Dumplings	1 cup	14
Full Bodied Vegetable with Beef Broth	1 cup	15
Golden Cream Chicken	1 cup	10
Hefty Vegetable with Ground Beef	1 cup	10
Hearty Vegetable Beef	1 cup	15
Luscious Split Pea with Smoked Ham	1 cup	15
Robust Chili Beef	1 cup	22
Savory Bean with Smoked Ham	1 cup	15
Tasty Turkey Noodle	1 cup	10
Tempting Chicken Rice with Mushrooms	1 cup	10
Velvety Cream of Mushroom	1 cup	13

Mixed Dishes

Brand	Product	Amount	Carbohydrate Grams
Campbell's	Barbecue Beans	¼ cup	15
	Beans and Franks in Tomato Sauce	¼ cup	7
	Beans 'n Beef in Tomato Sauce	¼ cup	7
	Pork/Beans/Tomato Sauce	¼ cup	15
Franco American	Italian Style Spaghetti	1 cup	30
	Macaroni and Cheese	1 cup	28
	Macaroni 'n Beef in Tomato Sauce	1 cup	22
	Macaroni O's with Cheese Sauce	1 cup	22
	Spaghetti O's with Sliced Franks	1 cup	30
	Spaghetti in Tomato Sauce/Cheese	1 cup	37
	Spaghetti 'n Beef in Tomato Sauce	1 cup	30
	Spaghetti O's in Tomato/Cheese Sauce	1 cup	37
	Spaghetti O's with Meatballs	1 cup	22
	Spaghetti with Meatballs	1 cup	22
Bounty	Beef Stew	1 cup	14
	Chicken Stew	1 cup	14
	Chili Con Carne	1 cup	22
	Corned Beef Hash	1 cup	14
Swanson	Chicken Pie	8 ounces	52
	Frozen Beef Pie	8 ounces	37
	Frozen Deep Dish Beef Pie	8 ounces	52
	Frozen Deep Dish Chicken Pie	8 ounces	52
	Frozen Deep Dish Turkey Pie	8 ounces	52
	Tuna Pie	8 ounces	37
	Turkey Pie	8 ounces	37

Cereals

Brand	Type	Amount	Carbohydrate Grams
General Mills	Cheerios	¾ cup	15
	Clackers	⅔ cup	15
	Cocoa Puffs	⅔ cup	15
	Corn Bursts	⅔ cup	15
	Country Corn Flakes	1 cup	15
	Frosty O's	½ cup	15
	Jets	½ cup	15
	Kix	1 cup	15
	Lucky Charms	¾ cup	15
	Stax	¾ cup	15
	Trix	⅔ cup	15
	Twinkles	⅔ cup	15
	Wheaties	⅔ cup	15
Kellogg's	All-Bran	⅓ cup	15
	Apple Jacks	⅔ cup	15
	Brand Buds	⅓ cup	15
	Cocoa Krispies	⅔ cup	15
	Corn Flakes	¾ cup	15
	40% Bran Flakes	½ cup	15
	Froot Loops	⅔ cup	15
	Krumbles	½ cup	15
	Pep Wheat Flakes	⅔ cup	15
	Product 19	⅔ cup	15

Brand	Type	Cereals	Amount	Carbohydrate Grams
Kellogg's	Puffa Puffa Rice		½ cup	15
	Raisin Bran		½ cup	15
	Rice Krispies		⅔ cup	15
	Shredded Wheat		1 biscuit	15
	Special K		¾ cup	15
	Stars		⅔ cup	15
Quaker	Captain Crunch		½ cup	15
	Diet Frosted Rice Puffs		½ cup	7
	Diet Frosted Wheat Puffs		¾ cup	7
	Instant Oatmeal		1 packet	22
	Instant Oatmeal with Apples and Cinnamon		1 packet	22
	Instant Oatmeal with Raisins and Spice		1 packet	30
	Life		½ cup	15
	Puffed Rice		¾ cup	7
	Puffed Wheat		¾ cup	7
	Quake		⅔ cup	15
	Quisp		¾ cup	15
	Shredded Wheat		1 biscuit	15

Frozen Foods

Brand	Type	Amount	Carbohydrate Grams
Aunt Jemima	Cinnamon Stick	1 stick	7
	Corn Sticks	1 stick	7
	Country Waffles	1 waffle	7
Kraft	Beef Ravioli	4 ounces	15
	Cheese Ravioli	4 ounces	15
	Macaroni and Cheese	4 ounces	15
	Spaghetti with Meat Sauce	4 ounces	15

Mixes

Brand	Type	Amount	Carbohydrate Grams
Aunt Jemima	Buckwheat Pancake and Waffle Mix	1 cake, 4" diameter	8
	Buttermilk Pancake and Waffle Mix	1 cake, 4" diameter	15
	Coffee Cake Easy Mix	1 piece (⅛ mix)	30
	Corn Bread Easy Mix	1 piece (⅛ mix)	37
	Deluxe Easy Pour Pancake and Waffle Mix	1 cake, 4" diameter	15
	Pancake and Waffle Mix	1 cake, 4" diameter	7
Flako	Corn Muffin Mix (12 per package)	1 muffin	22
	Cup Cake Mix (16 per package)	1 cup cake	15
	Pie Crust Mix	⅙ of a 9" pie crust	15
	Popover Mix (6 per package)	1 popover	22

Kosher Foods—Baker Products

Brand	Type	Amount	Carbohydrate Grams
Manischewitz	Diet Thins	per Matzo	22
	Egg (Passover) Matzo	per Matzo	30
	Egg 'n Onion	per Matzo	22
	Regular Unsalted	per Matzo	22
	Tasteas	per Matzo	22
	Thin Tea Matzo	per Matzo	22
	Whole Wheat Matzo (Passover)	per Matzo	22

Kosher Foods—Soup Products

Brand	Type	Amount	Carbohydrate Grams
Manischewitz	Bean Soup	8 ounces ready to eat	15
	Beef Barley Soup	8 ounces	15
	Beef Cabbage Soup	8 ounces	7
	Beef Noodle Soup	8 ounces	7
	Beef Vegetable Soup	8 ounces	7
	Borsch Soup	8 ounces	15
	Chicken Barley Soup	8 ounces	15
	Chicken Kasha	8 ounces	7
	Chicken Noodle Soup	8 ounces	7
	Chicken Rice Soup	8 ounces	7
	Chicken Vegetable Soup	8 ounces	7
	Lentil Soup	8 ounces	30

	Amount	Carbohydrate Grams
Lima Bean Soup	8 ounces	15
Mushroom Barley Soup	8 ounces	15
Schav Soup	no limit	0
Split Pea Soup	8 ounces	22
Tomato Rice Soup	8 ounces	15
Tomato Soup	8 ounces	15
Vegetarian Vegetable Soup	8 ounces	15

Others

Brand	Type	Amount	Carbohydrate Grams
Metrecal	Cookies (Cinnamon Snap, Chocolate, Chocolate Mint, Lemon Crisp)	9	34
	Diet Dinner (Chili Beans and Beef, Rice and Chicken, Spaghetti and Meat Sauce, Tuna and Noodles, Turkey and Noodles, Vegetables and Beef)	9 ounces	30
	Liquid (Chocolate, Vanilla)	8 ounces	27

Artificial Sweeteners

Saccharin

¼ grain	1 teaspoon sugar

Sprinkle Sweet

1 teaspoon	1 teaspoon sugar
2 teaspoons	2 teaspoons sugar
1 tablespoon	1 tablespoon sugar
¼ cup	¼ cup sugar
⅓ cup	⅓ cup sugar
½ cup	½ cup sugar

Sucaryl

⅛ teaspoon	1 teaspoon sugar
⅜ teaspoon	1 tablespoon sugar
1 teaspoon	8 teaspoons sugar
1½ teaspoons	¼ cup sugar
2 teaspoons	⅓ cup sugar
1 tablespoon	½ cup sugar
2 tablespoons	1 cup sugar

Sweet 10 (liquid)

⅛ teaspoon	1 teaspoon sugar
¼ teaspoon	2 teaspoons sugar
⅜ teaspoons	1 tablespoon sugar
1½ teaspoons	¼ cup sugar
2 teaspoons	⅓ cup sugar
1 tablespoon	½ cup sugar

Sweet & Low

1 packet	2 teaspoons sugar
3 packets	2 tablespoons sugar
6 packets	¼ cup sugar
12 packets	½ cup sugar
24 packets	1 cup sugar
3 teaspoons	½ cup sugar
6 teaspoons	1 cup sugar

Beverages

HOT SPICED TEA

4 cups water	juice of one lemon or more
¼ teaspoon cinnamon	if desired
¼ teaspoon nutmeg	½ cup orange juice
¼ teaspoon whole cloves	3 tablespoons tea, blended
1 tablespoon Sucaryl solution	

Boil together water, cinnamon, nutmeg, cloves, and Sucaryl solution for 10 minutes. Remove from flame and pour over tea which has been placed in teapot and allowed to steep 5 minutes. Strain. Add orange and lemon juices. To serve, reheat to boiling point. 4 servings. *1 serving contains 4 grams carbohydrate.*

HOT CHOCOLATE

3 cups milk	few grains salt
1½ unsweetened squares chocolate	1 teaspoon Sucaryl solution
	1 cup water, boiling

Scald milk. Melt chocolate in a saucepan over hot water. Add salt, Sucaryl solution and, gradually, boiling water. When smooth, place over direct heat and boil 5 minutes. Add scalded milk, beat with rotary beater and serve. A tablespoon of whipped cream may be used to garnish serving. 4 servings. *1 serving contains 12 grams carbohydrate.*

Spicy Hot Chocolate: Add two small cinnamon sticks and 10 whole cloves when adding salt and Sucaryl solution to the above recipe. Strain before adding scalded milk.

Minted Chocolate: Add two or three drops of peppermint extract to Hot Chocolate recipe and garnish with mint sprigs.

HOT SPICED CIDER

1 quart cider, sweet	¼ stick cinnamon
¼ teaspoon allspice	1 teaspoon Sucaryl solution
¼ teaspoon cloves	

Heat all ingredients in a saucepan and let simmer for 10 minutes. Strain and serve. 6 servings. *1 serving contains 20 grams carbohydrate.*

COCOA

3 tablespoons cocoa	3 cups milk
¼ teaspoon salt	6 Sucaryl tablets or ¾ teaspoon solution
1 cup water	

Mix cocoa and salt in top of double boiler. Add water, place over low heat; boil 2 minutes, stirring constantly. Add milk and Sucaryl tablets or solution, and heat over simmering water, stirring occasionally. For a frothy drink beat with a rotary beater just before serving. 4 servings. *1 serving contains 12 grams carbohydrate.*

MILKSHAKE

| ¼ cup powdered skim milk | 8 ounces low calorie carbonated creme, black-cherry, grape or coffee beverages |

Place powdered milk into blender. Pour carbonated beverage over powdered milk and blend at high speed for about 2 minutes. Serve in tall glasses. 1 serving. *1 serving contains 12 grams carbohydrate.*

LEMONADE

2½ Sucaryl tablets or ⅜ teaspoon of solution	6 ounces water
2 tablespoons fresh, strained lemon juice	1 slice lemon
	ice

Place Sucaryl tablets or solution in lemon juice. Add 6 ounces or 8 ounces of water. Add ice. Garnish with slice of lemon. 1 serving. Carbohydrate does not need to be considered.

COCKTAIL

| soda water | juice of ½ lemon |
| 1 maraschino cherry | artificial sweetener if desired |

Mix the lemon juice with a glass of soda water. Garnish with maraschino cherry. Sweeten with Sucaryl or saccharin as desired. 1 serving. Carbohydrate does not need to be considered.

PUNCH

1 quart apple cider	1 cup orange juice
1 cup unsweetened apricot or pineapple juice	1¼ tablespoons Sucaryl solution
½ cup lemon juice	1 quart ginger ale, dry

Combine cider, apricot juice, lemon juice, orange juice, and Sucaryl solution. Chill. When ready to serve add cold ginger ale and garnish with orange and lemon slices. 25 servings. *1 serving contains 10 grams carbohydrate.*

POP FROSTS

1 bottle sugar-free, saccharin or Sucaryl sweetened pop, any flavor	½ cup ice cream, vanilla

Place ice cream in a cold glass and add pop gradually, mixing with a spoon and using just enough pop to give desired consistency for the drink. Some will prefer less pop in order to have a thicker drink. *1 serving contains 15 grams carbohydrate.*

Appetizers and Relishes

APPETIZERS

celery sticks

carrots sticks

cherry tomatoes

radish roses

dill pickles

cucumber sliced

cauliflowerettes

Carbohydrate does not need to be considered.

GREEN ONION DIP

Combine 1 cup cottage cheese in blender with 2 table-spoons milk.

Variations: Add salt and pepper and chives to taste. Or add a commercial green onion dip mixed to blended cottage cheese to taste. Delicious with vegetable frills. Carbohydrate does not need to be considered.

CURRY DIP

1 cup cottage cheese blended in blender	2 teaspoons minced onion
	½ teaspoon salt
2 teaspoons curry powder	1 tablespoon lemon juice
½ teaspoon Tabasco sauce	

Mix ingredients and serve. 1 cup. Carbohydrate does not need to be considered.

DEVILED EGGS

6 hard cooked eggs	dash of Worcestershire
1 teaspoon mustard	sauce
salt and pepper to taste	1 tablespoon mayonnaise

Cut eggs in half. Scoop out yolks. Cream yolks with fork and mix with mustard and dressing. Season. Fill eggs and garnish with paprika. Carbohydrate does not need to be considered.

STUFFED CELERY

Whip cottage cheese until creamy. Place in refrigerator until firm. Use pastry bag to fill celery. Garnish with paprika or minced parsley. Carbohydrate does not need to be considered.

HOT STUFFED MUSHROOMS

mushroom caps	1 cup cottage cheese
½ cup canned mushroom slices	2 tablespoons chopped onions
1 teaspoon bouillon dissolved in 3 tablespoons hot water	dash of pepper

Put all ingredients except mushroom caps in blender and blend until just combined, not homogenized. Fill mushroom caps with mixture and bake at 350 degrees for 15 minutes. Serve hot. Carbohydrate does not need to be considered.

SPANISH SANDWICH SPREAD

¼ pound American cheese	2 tablespoons prepared
3 pimientoes	mustard
1 tablespoon horseradish	½ teaspoon salt
⅛ teaspoon paprika	2 hard boiled eggs
1 small onion	

Put through food chopper and mix well. This may be served as stuffing for celery. Carbohydrate does not need to be considered.

TUNA CANAPÉ

⅛ pound butter	1 teaspoon Worcestershire
2 tablespoons chopped onion	sauce
	½ teaspoon dry mustard
2 tablespoons mayonnaise	garlic salt
1 teaspoon lemon juice	1 small can tuna

Melt the butter or soften in a Waring blender mixer. Add the remaining ingredients to it. Grind all till smooth. Pour into small buttered bowl and freeze. Run hot water on bowl to unmold. Garnish with sliced stuffed olives and serve with thinly sliced ice box rye bread. You must let this stand before serving so that it isn't too hard to spread. Carbohydrate does not need to be considered.

OYSTER OR SHRIMP COCKTAIL SAUCE

1½ 14-ounce bottles of catsup	6 tablespoons Worcestershire sauce
½ 12-ounce bottle chili sauce	1 cup horseradish
	few dashes Tabasco sauce

Mix ingredients well, let stand 1 day to blend flavors. 1 quart. Carbohydrate does not need to be considered.

COCKTAIL-ARTICHOKE HEARTS AND DRESSING

¼ cup cream
¼ cup mayonnaise
¼ cup chili sauce

1 large can artichoke hearts

Beat cream until stiff. Beat in mayonnaise and chili sauce. Cut artichokes in small pieces. Mix with dressing. Chill and serve in small glasses. This has to be served immediately upon opening the can of artichokes. If artichokes stand they will get black. Carbohydrate does not need to be considered.

CLAM CANAPÉ OR DIP

Combine one small can of drained minced clams with two 3-ounce packages of soft cream cheese. Season with Worcestershire sauce, onion juice, and salt to taste. Use as a spread or thin with cream or clam juice to make soft enough for a dip. Carbohydrate does not need to be considered.

CHEESE ROLL

1 pound Roquefort cheese
¼ pound Old English cheese
½ cup finely chopped onions
1 cup chopped parsley

6 packages Philadelphia Cream Cheese
1½ tablespoons Worcestershire sauce
salt and pepper to taste
1 cup pecans, chopped

Soften cheese, add other ingredients using ½ parsley. Form in rolls; roll in rest of parsley. Chill. Serve in roll or slices. Carbohydrate does not need to be considered.

ROQUEFORT CELERY STICKS

6 good sized uniform celery sticks	6 drops Worcestershire sauce
½ pound Roquefort cheese	¼ teaspoon paprika
1 tablespoon salad oil	1 tablespoon butter

Mix ingredients thoroughly. Fill celery sticks with the mixture. Carbohydrate does not need to be considered.

CHEESE DIP

Camembert or Roquefort cheese spread; add cream as needed for consistency. Add juice from chopped onion, a few drops of Tabasco and Worcestershire, salt to taste. Sprinkle paprika on top of finished mixture. If made ahead of time and placed in refrigerator, beat in more cream to required consistency just before serving and renew paprika. Carbohydrate does not need to be considered.

STUFFED CELERY

Clean the celery stalks and wipe dry. Stuff with Philadelphia cream cheese mixed with chopped walnuts or pecans or sunflower seeds. Carbohydrate does not need to be considered.

RELISHES

Relishes are more appetizing when completely chilled and crisp. They should be prepared an hour or so before serving and kept in the refrigerator. Because of the loss of water-soluble minerals and vitamins, vegetables should not be allowed to stand in water for several hours.

Radishes: Wash carefully. Remove tips and leaves, retaining enough of stem for attractive appearance. To make radish roses, cut strips to resemble petals from the tip end toward the stem, being careful not to break off the cut portion. Keep in ice water until serving.

Celery: Wash carefully. Serve hearts whole or in individual stalks. To prepare celery curls, cut each stalk lengthwise in strips and immerse in ice water until serving.

Carrots: Wash and scrape. Cut thin strips, and chill thoroughly. Thin strips will curl if put immediately into ice water.

Cucumber: Wash and chill. Cucumbers may be peeled or not, as desired. Slice thinly. It serrated edges are desired, pull silver fork lengthwise along peeled cucumber to make parallel grooves; thin slice.

Carbohydrate does not need to be considered.

CRANBERRY RELISH

1 pound or 4 cups cranberries	1 unpeeled apple
1 orange	sweetener (as desired) using the artificial sweetener

Grind all fruits together in a food chopper. Add the noncaloric sweetener in the amount desired. Mix well and chill. Serve with lettuce. 8 servings. *1 serving contains 10 grams carbohydrate.* When used as a relish to accompany meats and fowl, the carbohydrate does not need to be considered.

CRANBERRY-ORANGE RELISH

2 cups cranberries	2 tablespoons Sucaryl solution
1 orange	

Wash and sort cranberries. Remove seeds from orange. Put both through the fine blade of a food chopper. Blend in the Sucaryl. Chill well before serving. 8 servings. *1 serving contains 5 grams carbohydrate.*

CUCUMBERS IN VINAIGRETTE

2 large cucumbers, thinly sliced
4 cups salted ice water
2 or 3 fresh green onions, chopped
½ teaspoon salt
¼ teaspoon pepper
1 teaspoon liquid Sucaryl sweetener
½ cup vinegar

In large mixing bowl, combine cucumbers and salted ice water; let stand for 30 minutes. Drain. Add onion. Combine remaining ingredients and mix well. Pour over cucumbers, tossing lightly. Cover, then chill several hours, stirring occasionally. Makes 8 (½) cup servings. Carbohydrate does not need to be considered.

Soups

JELLIED CONSOMMÉ

1 tablespoon unflavored
   gelatin
2 cups well-seasoned soup
   stock or consommé

sliced lemon
minced parsley

Soften gelatin in ¼ cup stock. Heat remainder of stock and stir into gelatin. Chill. When set, beat lightly with a fork and serve in soup cups. Serve each with slice of lemon dipped in parsley. 3 or 4 servings. Carbohydrate does not need to be considered.

CONSOMMÉ À LA MADRILÈNE

Follow directions for jellied consommé (above), substituting 1 cup stock or consommé. Add ⅓ cup tomato juice. If a highly seasoned madrilène is desired, add Worcestershire sauce and Tabasco to taste. Serve sprinkled with finely cut Pascal celery or green pepper. Place wedge of lemon on side of plate. Carbohydrate does not need to be considered.

CHINESE EGG SOUP

2 cups clear, seasoned
   broth (chicken or
   meat)

1 egg, beaten
1 teaspoon chopped parsley
   (fresh or dry)

Heat broth. While it is boiling, pour in beaten egg slowly, stirring constantly. Add parsley and serve. 2 servings. Carbohydrate does not need to be considered.

GREEN PEA SOUP

½ cup peas, cooked,
   canned, or infant,
   strained

1 cup beef broth or
   bouillon
salt and pepper to taste

Puree cooked or canned peas in a blender. Heat the broth and add it to the strained peas and reheat. Season to taste. One strip of bacon may be fried, diced and added to the soup. *1 serving contains 7 grams carbohydrate.*

FISH CHOWDER

1 teaspoon fat
½ small onion, chopped
1 small potato, diced

¼ or ½ cup cooked fish
   (1 or 2 ounces)
1 cup milk
salt and pepper to taste

Cook fish in salted water. Melt fat in saucepan, brown the onion. Add cooked fish, diced potato, ½ cup water in which fish was cooked. Cover and cook for 15 minutes until potatoes are tender. Add milk and seasonings. *1 serving contains 30 grams carbohydrate.*

VEGETABLE SOUP

1 cup meat stock or bouillon cube and 1 cup water	½ small onion, chopped
	¼ cup cabbage, shredded
	1 stalk celery, diced
½ cup mixed vegetables (carrots, peas)	¼ cup tomato juice
	salt and pepper to taste

Prepare vegetables and add to broth. Add tomato juice and salt and pepper. Boil together until vegetables are just tender, about 20 minutes. *1 serving contains 7 grams carbohydrate.*

SCOTCH BARLEY SOUP

5 to 6 pounds soup meat	4 onions
8 quarts water	1 or 2 garlic buds, cut up
⅓ cup salt	

Cook the above together for 6 to 8 hours. Adding more water as needed to keep to an 8 quart level. Remove bone, gristle, and fat. If you have time, let cool and remove all the fat. Leave meat in liquid. Add 1 parsnip cut fine and 1½ cups barley. Let cook about 1 hour. Add 6 to 8 onions, sliced; 1 parsnip, cut fine; 2 bunches of carrots, cut up; 3 or 4 potatoes, cut up. Cook about 20 minutes longer. Season to taste for serving. May freeze any unused soup. 10 servings. *1 serving contains 15 grams carbohydrate.*

Sauces

BARBECUE SAUCE I

1 quart cooked tomatoes	dash of Tabasco sauce
1 large onion	1 green pepper, chopped
2 cloves garlic	½ cup celery, chopped
juice of 3 lemons	½ cup salad oil
1 teaspoon Worcestershire sauce	salt to taste
	1 tablespoon brown sugar

Combine all ingredients and cook gently twenty minutes, then strain. Especially good for outdoor barbecuing. Carbohydrate does not need to be considered.

BARBECUE SAUCE II

2 teaspoons shortening	1½ cups sugar
½ medium onion, chopped	1 teaspoon salt
2 cups tomato juice	½ bottle catsup (about ¾ cup)
1 cup vinegar	2 teaspoons chili powder
1 teaspoon barbecue spice	little Worcestershire sauce

Fry onions in shortening. Add other ingredients and boil till thick. When used in small amounts the carbohydrate does not need to be considered. *2 tablespoons contains 6 grams carbohydrate.*

BARBECUE SAUCE III

1 cup tomato juice	1 teaspoon dehydrated onion flakes
1 envelope powdered mix for chicken broth	½ teaspoon paprika
3 tablespoons lemon juice or vinegar	dash coarse pepper
2 tablespoons Worcestershire sauce	dash cayenne pepper
1 clove garlic	½ envelope granulated sugar substitute or substitute for 1 teaspoon sugar
¾ teaspoon dry mustard	

Heat all the ingredients in a saucepan until thickened. Use as a baste on chicken. Carbohydrate does not need to be considered.

MORNAY SAUCE

1 tablespoon butter or margarine	2 tablespoons flour
1 teaspoon minced or finely sliced onion	1 cup skim milk
	¼ cup shredded Swiss or Gruyere cheese

Melt butter in skillet. Add onion and cook until onion is

yellow. Add flour, cook until mixture bubbles. Slowly stir in milk. Cook over low heat until thickened and smooth. Add ¼ cup shredded cheese; cook, stirring until cheese is melted. *1 serving contains 21 grams carbohydrate.*

RUM SAUCE

1 cup evaporated skimmed milk	⅛ teaspoon salt
2 eggs	1 teaspoon rum flavor
½ teaspoon liquid sweetener (artificial)	

Mix thoroughly. Heat. Serve hot over fruit. Makes 2 cups. Up to ¼ cup the carbohydrate does not need to be considered.

PROPORTIONS FOR WHITE SAUCES
(1 cup)

Consistency	Cups of Milk	Tbsp. Fat	Tbsp. Flour	Tsp. Salt
Very thin	1	½	½	½
Thin	1	1	1	½
Medium	1	2	2	½
Thick	1	3	3	½

Melt the fat in top of double boiler, and mix in the salt and flour to make a smooth paste. Add liquid gradually to the flour mixture and continue stirring until thickened sufficiently. Cover, and cook for 10 to 15 minutes, stirring from time to time. The sauce may also be made by melting fat in saucepan over direct heat. Add flour and stir until smooth. Add liquid gradually, stir constantly and cook over low heat until sauce comes to a boil.

Very thin sauce—*1 cup contains 9 grams carbohydrate.*
Thin sauce—*1 cup contains 18 grams carbohydrate.*
Medium sauce—*1 cup contains 24 grams carbohydrate.*
Thick sauce—*1 cup contains 30 grams carbohydrate.*

SOFT CUSTARD

2 cups milk
3 egg yolks
⅛ teaspoon salt

½ teaspoon vanilla
  extract
1½ teaspoons Sucaryl
  solution

Scald milk. Place egg yolks in the top of a double boiler and beat slightly with a fork. Add salt. While stirring constantly, add hot milk gradually and cook until mixture forms a coating on the spoon. Add vanilla and Sucaryl solution, strain, and cool. 6 servings. *1 serving contains 4 grams carbohydrate.*

CHOCOLATE SAUCE

½ cup cocoa
½ teaspoon salt
1½ cups evaporated milk

1½ teaspoons Sucaryl
  solution
½ teaspoon vanilla
  extract

Mix together cocoa and salt in top of double boiler. Add evaporated milk gradually, stirring constantly in order to keep mixture smooth. Cook over hot water until thick. Add Sucaryl solution and vanilla. Pour into a glass jar and keep in refrigerator. 10 servings or 20 tablespoons. *2 tablespoons contains 6 grams carbohydrate.*

NOTE: A few drops of peppermint or almond or pineapple flavoring may be used in place of the vanilla.

WHIPPED TOPPING

½ cup skim milk powder
¼ cup fruit juice or water

vanilla, lemon, almond etc.
  flavoring extract to
  taste
Sucaryl solution to taste

Combine milk powder with ¼ cup liquid (all fruit juice or part fruit juice and part water). Add extra flavoring and Sucaryl solution, if desired. Beat until fluffy. Topping will thicken, if allowed to stand. 8 servings. *1 serving contains 4 grams carbohydrate.* If used as topping or garnish, the carbohydrate does not need to be considered.

NOTE: For a cocoa flavor try mixing a teaspoon cocoa with milk powder and combining with ¼ cup water.

CHERRY SAUCE

1 tablespoon cornstarch
2 tablespoons water
¾ cup hot cherry juice (left from canned water-packed fruit)

½ teaspoon Sucaryl solution
⅛ teaspoon almond extract

Blend cornstarch with water. Add hot cherry juice and Sucaryl solution. Boil three minutes. Add almond flavoring. Serve warm. One serving contains little carbohydrate and does not need to be considered.

BLUEBERRY SAUCE

1 pound can water-packed blueberries or fresh blueberries
2 teaspoons cornstarch

1 teaspoon lemon juice
artificial sweetener to taste, use sparingly

Cook and stir blueberries and 2 teaspoons cornstarch until mixture thickens. Add artificial sweetener and lemon juice. 1 cup.

1 tablespoon does not need to be considered for carbohydrate.

2 tablespoons contains 5 grams carbohydrate.

¼ cup contains 10 grams carbohydrate.

NOTE: If you desire to use low calorie syrup, the same carbohydrate content applies.

LEMON SAUCE

1 tablespoon cornstarch
2 tablespoons cold water
1 cup boiling water
2 teaspoons margarine
2 tablespoons lemon juice

2 teaspoons Sucaryl solution
few grains salt
nutmeg, few gratings

Blend cornstarch with cold water. Add boiling water and boil 5 minutes, stirring constantly. Remove from fire and add margarine, lemon juice, Sucaryl solution, salt, and nutmeg. 8 servings. Carbohydrate does not need to be considered.

NOTE: For vanilla sauce use 1 teaspoon vanilla instead of lemon juice. For maple syrup use ½ teaspoon imitation maple flavoring instead of lemon juice and nutmeg.

CREAMY MAPLE DESSERT SAUCE

¼ cup margarine or butter
2 tablespoons flour
2 tablespoons liquid
Sucaryl

½ cup water
1 cup evaporated milk
1½ teaspoons maple
flavoring

Melt margarine; blend in flour; add Sucaryl, water, and milk. Cook over medium heat, stirring constantly until thickened. Remove from heat and add flavoring. Chill. Makes 1½ cups. *¼ cup contains 6 grams carbohydrate.*

MINT SAUCE

¼ cup water
artificial sweetener equal to
1 tablespoon sugar

¼ cup finely chopped mint
leaves
½ cup malt vinegar

Make the mint sauce in advance. Combine the water and artificial sweetener in saucepan, bring to boil. Remove from heat and stir in the mint leaves and vinegar. Taste and add more artificial sweetener if desired. Set aside at room temperature for 2 or 3 hours. Delicious with leg of lamb. Carbohydrate does not need to be considered.

MUSHROOM SAUCE

3 tablespoons margarine
1½ cups mushrooms
3 tablespoons flour
1½ cups skim milk, scalded
salt and pepper to taste

Brown margarine and mushrooms in a saucepan. While stirring contantly, add flour and then scalded milk, salt, and pepper. Cook until thick. Serve. 4 servings. *1 serving contains 9 grams carbohydrate.*

SEAFOOD COCKTAIL SAUCE

½ cup tomato juice
1 teaspoon prepared horseradish
1 teaspoon lemon juice
½ teaspoon Worcestershire sauce
½ teaspoon salt
½ teaspoon finely chopped parsley
any other desired seasonings

Cook tomato juice down to half its volume. Mix additional ingredients with tomato juice. Serve with shrimp or other cooked seafood. Carbohydrate does not need to be considered.

SWEET AND SOUR SAUCE

5 tablespoons lemon juice
¾ cup water
1 tablespoon soy sauce
1 clove garlic, cut in several pieces
artificial sweetener to replace 1 teaspoon sugar
1 2"-square of pimiento, finely diced

In saucepan, combine all ingredients. Cook for ten minutes, uncovered. Discard garlic. Use for fruit salad, with Chinese dishes, or for basting chicken or pork. Carbohydrate does not need to be considered.

Salad Dressings

Salad dressings may be stored in a refrigerator for future use, and therefore quantities larger than individual portions may be prepared. Dressings to which other foods have been added, as in Russian or Thousand Island dressings, should be mixed just before use.

FRENCH DRESSING

½ cup salad oil
¼ cup lemon juice or
     vinegar
1 teaspoon salt

¼ teaspoon dry mustard
few drops onion juice
dash paprika

Put ingredients in glass jar and shake thoroughly. Chill. Carbohydrate does not need to be considered.

FRENCH DRESSING

1 cup salad oil
¼ to ⅓ cup lemon juice or vinegar

½ teaspoon salt
½ teaspoon paprika
⅛ teaspoon red pepper

Add dry ingredients to oil and lemon juice in jar. Cover closely and shake briskly until emulsified, or place in a deep bowl and beat well with a rotary beater. If the dressing is not to be used at once, shake well before serving. Carbohydrate does not need to be considered.

Variations: (1) add 1½ teaspoons onion juice and 2½ teaspoons Worcestershire sauce to 1 cup French dressing; (2) add 1 finely chopped pimiento, ½ green pepper, and 1 green onion.

ROQUEFORT DRESSING

½ teaspoon salt
½ teaspoon dry mustard
½ teaspoon paprika
few grains cayenne
2 tablespoons lemon juice
2 tablespoons vinegar

½ cup salad oil
¼ cup Roquefort or Blue cheese, crumbled
½ teaspoon Worcestershire sauce (optional)

Put all ingredients in jar. Cover. Shake well before using. Carbohydrate does not need to be considered.

MAYONNAISE I

1 egg yolk
½ teaspoon mustard, dry
½ teaspoon salt
few grains cayenne
⅛ teaspoon Sucaryl solutions

1 cup salad oil
1 tablespoon vinegar
1 tablespoon lemon juice
onion or garlic juice, as desired

Beat egg yolk until thick. Add mustard, salt, cayenne,

Sucaryl solution. While beating constantly add salad oil, 1 teaspoon at a time, alternately with vinegar and lemon juice until all have been added. Add onion juice or garlic if desired. Carbohydrate does not need to be considered.

MAYONNAISE II

1 egg yolk or 1 whole egg	1½ tablespoons lemon
¼ teaspoon dry mustard	juice or vinegar
½ teaspoon salt	1 cup salad oil

Mix dry ingredients with egg. Add lemon juice and stir well. With a rotary beater, beat in oil a few drops at a time until the mixture begins to thicken, then add in gradually larger quantities. Beat until stiff. If whole egg is used, increase salad oil to 1½ cups. The emulsion may break because of too rapid addition of oil or incontinuous beating. If this occurs, beat an egg yolk in a clean bowl, and add the broken emulsion drop by drop until completely added; then continue to add the remainder of the oil. Carbohydrate does not need to be considered.

Variations: (1) add ½ cup Roquefort cheese to 1 cup of mayonnaise; (2) mix equal quantities of whipped cream and mayonnaise.

GARLIC DRESSING

1 clove garlic, finely chopped	1 tablespoon cheneys choice
⅔ cup salad oil	¼ teaspoon paprika
¼ cup garlic vinegar	⅛ teaspoon salt
⅛ teaspoon Beaumonde seasoning	

Shake all ingredients in glass jar. Let stand two hours or more before using. Carbohydrate does not have to be considered.

RUSSIAN DRESSING

1 cup salad oil
artificial sweetener to equal
    ½ cup sugar
½ cup vinegar
½ cup catsup

dash of pepper
1 onion grated
½ clove garlic
½ teaspoon paprika
1 teaspoon salt

Mix all ingredients together with rotary egg beater. Shake before using. Carbohydrate does not need to be considered.

ZERO SALAD DRESSING

½ cup tomato juice
2 tablespoons lemon juice
    or vinegar
chopped parsley, if desired
horseradish, if desired
1 tablespoon onion, finely
    chopped

salt and pepper to taste
green pepper, chopped, if
    desired
mustard, if desired

Combine ingredients in a jar with a tightly fitted top. Shake well before using. Carbohydrate does not need to be considered.

COOKED DRESSING

2 tablespoons flour
artificial sweetener equal to
    1 tablespoon sugar
1 teaspoon salt
½ teaspoon dry mustard
⅛ teaspoon red pepper

¾ cup hot water
¼ cup mild vinegar
1 egg
2 tablespoons margarine
    or butter

Mix flour and seasonings. Slowly add liquid. Add artificial sweetener. Cook until thickened, stirring constantly. Add vinegar and blend well. Pour mixture over slightly beaten egg and cook for 1 to 2 minutes longer. Add margarine and cool before using. Yields 1½ cups. Carbohydrate does not need to be considered for small servings as the total recipe is 12 grams carbohydrate.

TWENTY-FOUR HOUR SALAD DRESSING FOR FRUIT SALAD

2 eggs, beaten
artificial sweetener equal to
   2 teaspoons sugar

¼ cup coffee cream
juice of 1 lemon
1 cup whipped cream

Boil the beaten egg with the artificial sweetener, coffee cream, and lemon juice until thick. Cool. Add whipped cream. Carbohydrate does not need to be considered.

Salads

MIXED GREEN SALAD

Use a combination of well-dried, crisp and thoroughly chilled greens such as watercress, lettuce, romaine, chicory, endive, escarole, spinach, dandelion, or beet greens. Finely sliced radishes, cucumbers, carrots or tomatoes, cauliflowerettes and sometimes fine cuts of ham, cheese, turkey, chicken, or crumbled crisp bacon are used with the greens. Tear greens into small pieces before putting into wooden bowl. Pour French dressing over greens and toss lightly with two forks until greens are well coated with dressing. Serve immediately. Carbohydrate does not need to be considered.

MIXED VEGETABLE SALAD COMBINATIONS

lettuce, cucumber, celery, green pepper

chicory, tomato, radish, grated carrot

lettuce, parsley, raw cauliflower, tomato

escarole, tomato, cucumber, string beans

cabbage, celery, green pepper, grated carrot

lettuce, watercress, cucumber, cooked peas

lettuce, raw spinach, radish

Salads may be combined with French dressing or mayonnaise. Carbohydrate does not need to be considered.

CUCUMBER BOAT

¼ cup flaked fish, shrimp, or crabmeat

¼ cup chopped celery or green pepper

salad dressing

Mix fish, vegetables, and dressing. Add salt to taste. Peel cucumber, cut lengthwise in half and scoop out center. Fill with fish mixture. Garnish with strip of pimiento or parsley. 2 servings. Carbohydrate does not need to be considered.

STUFFED TOMATO

1 medium tomato

⅛ teaspoon salt

1 tablespoon diced cucumber

1 tablespoon diced celery

1 tablespoon chopped green pepper

2 teaspoons mayonnaise

Remove skin from tomato. Cut slice from top and remove pulp, sprinkle inside with salt, and allow to drain. Fill cavity with mixture of cucumber, celery, green pepper, tomato pulp and 1 teaspoon of mayonnaise. Place on lettuce and garnish with thinly sliced rings of pepper and mayonnaise. Carbohydrate does not need to be considered.

SHREDDED CARROT AND CABBAGE SALAD

¼ cup shredded cabbage   **French dressing**
¼ cup shredded carrots   **salad greens**

Marinate cabbage and carrots with dressing for about 1 hour. Serve on salad greens. Carbohydrate does not need to be considered.

MARINATED BEAN SALAD

1 can (1 pound) cut green beans
1 can (1 pound) cut yellow beans
½ cup cider vinegar
2 teaspoons liquid sweetener

1 teaspoon mixed pickling spices
1 cup thinly sliced celery
1 small onion, chopped
2 tablespoons chopped green pepper
2 tablespoons chopped pimiento

Drain beans; reserve ½ cup liquid. In large mixing bowl, combine reserved ½ cup liquid, vinegar, liquid sweetener, and spices. Add beans and remaining ingredients. Mix well. Cover. Chill overnight, stirring occasionally. Store in refrigerator. Makes 12 (½ cup servings). If you wish to remove the mixed pickling spices before serving, tie them in a piece of cheesecloth before adding to vinegar. For 6 servings, use 8-ounce cans of beans and half of the other ingredients. *½ cup serving contains 5 grams carbohydrate.*

COLE SLAW

⅓ cup shredded cabbage
2 tablespoons salad dress-
      ing or mayonnaise
¼ cup shredded carrot

1 tablespoon finely cut
      celery
1 teaspoon finely cut
      parsley

Combine all ingredients well. Chill before serving. 1 serving. Carbohydrate does not need to be considered.

COLE SLAW

1 slice bacon
1 tablespoon vinegar
2 cups shredded cabbage
½ cup diced celery

1 tablespoon chopped
      onion
¼ cup cooked dressing or
      mayonnaise
salt and pepper to taste

Cut bacon into small pieces and cook until crisp enough to crumble, taking care not to allow any pieces to burn. Add vinegar to bacon. Pour over cabbage, celery, and onion and mix lightly. Add cooked dressing or mayonnaise and salt and pepper. This makes a hearty salad by the addition of a hard cooked egg. Carbohydrate does not need to be considered.

RED CABBAGE SALAD

Grate red cabbage, crumble Roquefort cheese all through it. Put it on salad plates and put this dressing on it. (Excellent with game.)

1 egg, beaten
1 cup salad oil
¼ cup vinegar
artificial sweetener equal to
      ¼ cup sugar

1 teaspoon dry mustard
1 teaspoon salt
1 tablespoon celery salt
1 small onion grated

Carbohydrate does not need to be considered.

GREEN GODDESS SALAD

1 clove garlic, minced	3 tablespoons minced
½ teaspoon salt	chives or scallions
½ teaspoon dry mustard	⅓ cup snipped parsley
1 teaspoon Worcestershire	1 cup mayonnaise
sauce	½ cup commercial sour
2 tablespoons anchovy	cream
paste	⅛ teaspoon black pepper
3 tablespoons tarragon	1 quart salad greens
wine vinegar	

Day or two before serving: Combine all ingredients in a bowl, except the salad greens. Mix until well blended, then refrigerate, covered, until needed.

At serving time: Add about ⅓ cup of the refrigerated dressing to the salad greens. Toss well, then serve at once, garnish with stuffed olives if desired. 4 servings. The leftover dressing (about 1⅓ cups) keeps well several days in refrigerator. Carbohydrate does not need to be considered.

CELERY, CAULIFLOWER, AND TOMATO SALAD

1 cup celery, chopped	4 tomatoe slices
1½ cups cauliflower, raw,	8 tablespoons cottage
thinly sliced	cheese
½ cup French dressing	1 small head lettuce (1 cup)

Marinate celery and cauliflower in French dressing for half an hour. Drain. Arrange tomato slices on lettuce and place a serving of vegetable mixture on each. Top with cottage cheese. 4 servings. Carbohydrate does not need to be considered.

CRANBERRY SALAD

1 orange with rind
¼ lemon with rind
2 cups cranberries
1 apple, unpeeled,
    chopped
½ cup celery, chopped

½ cup pineapple wedges
¼ cup pecans, broken
1 teaspoon Sucaryl
    solution
1 small head lettuce

Grind orange, lemon, and cranberries through food chopper. Add apple, celery, pineapple, pecans, and Sucaryl solution. Mix well. Chill. Serve on lettuce leaves or other salad greens. 6 servings. *1 serving contains 9 grams carbohydrate.*

FRUIT MEDLEY SALAD

1 envelope (1 table-
    spoon) unflavored
    gelatin
½ cup unsweetened or-
    ange juice
1¼ cups boiling water
¼ teaspoon salt

1¼ teaspoons liquid
    sweetener
food coloring, if desired
1 medium pear or apple,
    diced
½ cup Tokay grapes, cut
    in half and seeded

In medium mixing bowl, soften gelatin in orange juice. Stir in boiling water, salt, and liquid sweetener. Chill until slightly thickened but not set. Carefully stir in fruit. Pour into a 3- or 4-cup mold or 6 individual molds. Chill until set, about 4 hours. 6 servings. *1 serving contains 10 grams carbohydrate.*

COMBINATION FRUIT SALAD

1 slice canned pineapple
2 sections grapefruit
6 white grapes or cherries

lettuce
mayonnaise
1 orange cut in sections

Dice pineapple, add shredded grapefruit and grapes or cherries. Mix with mayonnaise. Arrange small inner leaves of lettuce on a salad plate. Pile mixture in center of lettuce. Arrange orange sections about the fruit mixture. *1 serving contains 15 grams carbohydrate.*

WALDORF SALAD

1 apple (small)
2 tablespoons English walnuts

2 tablespoons diced celery
2 teaspoons mayonnaise
lettuce

Select firm tart apples. Pare, core and cut apple into ½" cubes. Break the walnuts into pieces. Mix the apple, walnuts, and celery together and add mayonnaise. Place upon lettuce leaves or other salad greens. *1 serving contains 10 grams carbohydrate.*

ORANGE AND GRAPEFRUIT SALAD

4 sections orange
3 sections grapefruit

lettuce or watercress
French dressing

Section fruit. Arrange alternate sections of orange and grapefruit on salad greens and serve with French dressing. 1 serving. Carbohydrate does not need to be considered.

CARROT-ORANGE TOSS SALAD

2 oranges, diced
2 cups grated carrot
½ cup raisins

2 tablespoons honey
1 teaspoon lemon juice

Combine all ingredients. Chill. Serve on lettuce cups. 6 servings. *1 serving contains 29 grams carbohydrate.* If artificial sweetener to equal 2 tablespoons of sugar or honey is used, *then 1 serving is 24 grams carbohydrate.*

FRUIT AND CHEESE SALAD

2 dried prunes, cooked   3 level tablespoons cottage
   without sugar   cheese
3 medium slices tomatoes   2 lettuce leaves

Place the three slices of tomato on lettuce leaves. Top
with cottage cheese. Place prunes on the side. Garnish with
chopped chives, watercress, or parsley. Serve with dressing.
1 serving contains 10 grams carbohydrate.

STUFFED-EGG SALAD

1 hard-cooked egg   lettuce leaves
1 teaspoon anchovy paste   mayonnaise
green pepper

Cut egg lengthwise. Mash yolk through sieve and add
anchovy paste and a little mayonnaise. Return yolk paste
to the white and arrange ou slices of green pepper. Place
on lettuce and serve with mayonnaise or any preferred salad
dressing. The anchovy paste may be omitted and the yolk
mixed with cream and mayonnaise and seasoned to taste.
Carbohydrate does not need to be considered.

COTTAGE CHEESE SALAD

⅓ cup cottage cheese   salad greens
1 teaspoon minced green   French dressing
   pepper   paprika

Mix cottage cheese with minced green pepper and serve
on lettuce or other greens with French dressing. Garnish
with paprika. The above cottage-cheese mixture may be
served with (1) sliced pineapple, halves of pear or peach,
as stuffing for prunes or apricots, or to accompany any fruit
salad; (2) sliced tomato or whole tomato stuffed with the
mixture. Carbohydrate does not need to be considered.

CAULIFLOWER-ROQUEFORT SALAD

1 clove garlic
2 cups raw cauliflower-
    ettes

½ cup Roquefort-type
    cheese, crumbled
1 head lettuce, shredded
¼ cup French dressing

Rub salad bowl with cut clove of garlic. Mix cauliflower-ettes, cheese, and lettuce in bowl. Add French dressing and toss lightly until ingredients are well mixed. Serve. 6 servings. Carbohydrate does not need to be considered.

SUNSET SALAD

1 envelope (4-serving size)
    low calorie orange
    gelatin dessert
⅛ teaspoon salt
2 cups boiling water
1 tablespoon vinegar

⅔ cup coarsely grated raw
    carrots
¼ cup diced drained un-
    sweetened pineapple
    (cooked or canned)

Dissolve gelatin and salt in boiling water. Add vinegar. Chill until thickened. Then fold in carrots and pineapple. Pour into molds. Chill until firm. Unmold on crisp salad greens. Serve with dressing if desired. Makes about 2 cups or 4 servings. *1 serving contains 5 grams carbohydrate.*

FRUIT GELATIN

1 envelope unflavored
    gelatin
¼ cup water
5 Sucaryl tablets

2 tablespoons lemon juice
2 cups unsweetened fruit
    juice

Soften gelatin in cold water for 5 minutes. Mash Sucaryl tablets and dissolve in 1 tablespoon of the fruit juice. Add to remaining fruit and lemon juices. Dissolve gelatin over hot water, add to fruit juices, blend. Pour into individual molds. Chill. 4 servings. *1 serving contains 10 grams carbohydrate.*

JELLIED SPRING VEGETABLE SALAD

1 tablespoon unflavored gelatin
¼ cup cold water
2 cups boiling water
½ teaspoon salt
¼ cup lime juice
2 teaspoons Sucaryl solution

few drops green food coloring
1 cup diced, peeled cucumber
1 cup sliced radishes
¼ cup sliced scallions or onion

Soften gelatin in cold water; dissolve in boiling water. Add salt, lime juice, Sucaryl, and coloring. Chill until mixture begins to thicken. Fold in remaining ingredients. Chill until set in a 5-cup mold. 8 servings. Carbohydrate does not need to be considered.

PINEAPPLE MOLD

1 package lime or strawberry flavored Dzerta gelatin
1 cup hot water

1 cup canned pineapple juice
⅛ teaspoon salt
1 egg white

Dissolve gelatin in hot water. Add the pineapple juice and salt. Chill until slightly thickened. Place in bowl of ice and water. Add the egg white, and whip with egg beater until fluffy and thick. Pile lightly in sherbet glasses. Chill until firm. 6 servings. Carbohydrate does not need to be considered.

CHICKEN-GRAPE SALAD

12 ounces chicken, cooked,   1 cup celery, diced
    cold, diced (1½   ¾ cup grape halves, seeded
    cups)   1 small head of lettuce
¼ cup French dressing

Marinate chicken for one-half hour in French dressing made with lemon juice. Combine chicken, celery, and grapes. Place mixture in lettuce cups and garnish with lemon slices. 4 servings. *1 serving contains 5 grams carbohydrate.*

CELERY-BANANA SALAD

½ cup lettuce   ½ small banana
1 large celery stick   1 teaspoon mayonnaise
1 tablespoon cream
    cheese

Stuff celery with cream cheese and then cut into small pieces. Arrange with sliced banana in lettuce cup and garnish with mayonnaise. 1 serving. *1 serving contains 10 grams carbohydrate.* NOTE: Peanut butter may be used in place of cream cheese.

FROZEN FRUIT SALAD

2 cups cherries, pitted   3 ounces cream cheese
½ cup pineapple, cubed   2 tablespoons mayonnaise
⅓ cup banana, sliced   dash salt
12 pecans, chopped   small head lettuce

Combine fruits and nuts. Blend together mayonnaise, cheese, and salt. Combine two mixtures thoroughly. Pack in refrigerator tray and freeze until firm. Serve on lettuce leaves. 6 servings. *1 serving contains 11 grams carbohydrate.*

TUNA VEGETABLE SALAD

1 cup carrots, cooked, diced	1 teaspoon salt
1 cup celery, chopped	dash pepper
1 cup green beans, cooked	1 tablespoon onion, grated
¼ cup French dressing	1 tablespoon parsley, chopped
1 can tuna fish	1 small head lettuce

Marinate carrots, celery and green beans in French dressing for one-half hour. Add remaining ingredients, except lettuce and toss lightly. Serve on lettuce leaves. 6 servings. Carbohydrate does not need to be considered.

TOMATO JELLY

1½ teaspoons granulated gelatin	3 cloves
2 tablespoons cold water	1 tablespoon minced parsley
1 cup canned tomatoes or tomato juice	½ teaspoon salt
2 tablespoons celery, diced	1 bay leaf
	1 tablespoon mild vinegar

Soak gelatin in cold water. Simmer remaining ingredients gently for 20 minutes. Press through a sieve and measure. Add water to make 1 cup liquid and bring to a boil. Pour over the soaked gelatin and stir until gelatin is dissolved. Pour into molds and chill until set. One or more of the following may be added when the jelly begins to thicken: finely chopped or sliced celery, green pepper, olives, carrots, or flaked fish. Carbohydrate does not need to be considered.

TOMATO ASPIC SEAFOOD SALAD
ASPIC

2 tablespoons plain
    gelatin
½ cup cold water
2½ cups tomato juice
1 teaspoon chopped
    onion

½ teaspoon salt
½ teaspoon celery salt
1 Sucaryl tablet
2 tablespoons vinegar

SALAD

1 cup tuna fish, flaked
1 cup diced celery
1 cup diced vegetables of
    choice
¼ teaspoon salt

dash white pepper
¼ cup mayonnaise
1 tablespoon lemon juice
grapefruit sections
watercress

Aspic: Soften gelatin in cold water. Combine tomato juice, onion, salt, celery salt, Sucaryl, and vinegar in saucepan; bring to boiling point. Add to gelatin, stirring until gelatin is dissolved. Strain mixture and pour into 1-quart ring mold. Chill until firm.

Salad: Lightly toss together tuna fish, celery, vegetables, salt, and pepper. Combine mayonnaise and lemon juice. Add to tuna fish mixture and blend carefully. Unmold aspic and fill center of ring with tuna fish salad. Arrange garnish of grapefruit sections and watercress around outer edge of aspic ring. 6 servings. Lobster, shrimp, or chicken may be substituted for tuna. Carbohydrate does not need to be considered.

POTATO SALAD I

½ cup cold, boiled, diced
   potato
2 tablespoons diced celery
1 tablespoon diced cu-
   cumber

1 tablespoon French
   dressing
1 tablespoon mayonnaise
lettuce
radishes, parsley, or hard
   boiled egg

Marinate potato, celery, and cucumber with French dressing. Before serving mix with cooked dressing and place on lettuce. Garnish with radishes, parsley, or hard boiled egg. *1 serving contains 15 grams carbohydrate.*

POTATO SALAD II

½ cup cooked potato,
   diced
salt and pepper to taste
chopped onion, as desired

chopped green pepper, as
   desired
2 tablespoons mayonnaise
chopped parsley, as desired

Combine all ingredients. Serve. *1 serving contains 15 grams carbohydrate.*

POTATO SALAD III

1 hard cooked egg, sliced, may be added to recipe for Potato Salad II. Variation is nice with ¼ cup (1 ounce) diced ham, bologna, or frankfurter or 5 small shrimp used in place of the egg. *1 serving contains 15 grams carbohydrate.*

JELLIED FISH SALAD

1 tablespoon unflavored gelatin	1 8-ounce can tuna fish, flaked
¼ cup cold water	2 tablespoons minced pickle or pepper relish
1½ cups boiling water	
½ teaspoon salt	
1 drop Sucaryl solution	¼ green pepper, minced
3 tablespoons vinegar	½ small onion, minced
	1 cup celery, minced

Soften gelatin in ¼ cup cold water. Add boiling water, salt, and Sucaryl, and stir until gelatin is dissolved. Add vinegar. Chill. When jelly is nearly set, stir in flaked fish, pickles, or relish, and minced vegetables. Pour into mold and chill until firm. Unmold and garnish with salad greens. Serve with dressing. 4 servings. Carbohydrate does not need to be considered.

NOTE: 1 cup canned shellfish or diced cooked meat or chicken may be substituted for the tuna fish.

CHICKEN AND MUSHROOM SALAD

2 ounces cooked or canned chicken, diced	½ cup diced celery
	2 teaspoons mayonnaise
½ cup cooked or drained canned mushrooms, stems and pieces	½ teaspoon lemon juice or vinegar
	salt and pepper to taste
	lettuce

Combine all ingredients and serve on lettuce. 1 serving. Carbohydrate does not need to be considered. Shrimp, tuna, salmon, or turkey may be substituted for the chicken.

FISH SALAD

⅓ cup shrimp, flaked
  salmon, tuna, crab-
  meat or lobster
⅓ cup diced celery
1 tablespoon French
  dressing

1 tablespoon mayonnaise
lettuce
½ hard boiled egg
½ tomato

Mix fish, celery, and French dressing. Chill for 1 hour and mix with mayonnaise. Serve on lettuce and garnish with slices of hard cooked egg and wedges of tomato. A whole tomato from which the pulp has been removed may be stuffed with the above mixture. Carbohydrate does not need to be considered.

Meat and Poultry

PORK ROAST WITH GRAVY

1 3-pound boneless pork
    loin roast
marinade, 1 cup stock
1 medium onion, thinly
    sliced

1 medium carrot, thinly
    sliced
¼ cup flour

Day before serving: Place pork in 12″ x 8″ baking dish with marinade; refrigerate covered, turning and basting occasionally.

About 3 hours before serving: Preheat oven to 325 **degrees.** Remove roast from marinade and place on rack in **shallow** open pan; reserve marinade. Insert meat thermometer into center of roast. Cook 2 hours or until thermometer reaches 170 degrees. Trim all fat from meat before serving.

About 20 minutes before serving: In medium covered saucepan over medium heat cook reserved marinade, onion, and carrot for 15 minutes, strain and return to saucepan. In a cup mix flour with ¼ cup cold water; stir into strained marinade. Cook over medium heat until thickened. Serve as gravy. Makes 8 servings. Carbohydrate does not need to be considered.

PORK CHOPS WITH BROWNED RICE

6 pork chops	1½ cups water
2 tablespoons fat	½ cup chopped green pepper
3 teaspoons salt	
1 cup uncooked rice	½ cup minced onion
2 cups tomatoes	¼ teaspoon pepper

Brown chops in fat, using a Dutch oven or any casserole dish that can be used on range and in the oven. Remove and season with 1 tablespoon salt. Wash the rice, then brown it in fat left in pan, stirring constantly. Add remaining of ingredients. Place chop on top. Bake 1¼ hours at 350 degrees. *½ cup rice contains 15 grams carbohydrate.*

PORK CHOPS AND RICE

6 pork chops	chopped celery
1 can tomato soup	chopped onion
salt, pepper, sage	bay leaf
curry powder	Worcestershire sauce

Season pork chops with salt, pepper, and sage. Lay flat in

bottom of large casserole. Cover each chop with a handful of dry rice, about one cup in all. Dilute soup and season highly with as much onion and celery as you like, bay leaf, Worcestershire sauce, and a little curry powder. Pour over chops and rice. Bake in a moderate oven 2 hours or more. *½ cup rice contains 15 grams carbohydrate.*

FRENCH BEEF-AND-VEGETABLE CASSEROLE

6 slices bacon
1 pound lean beef chuck, about ½ inch thick
½ cup flour
1 teaspoon salt
1 cup dry red wine
2 tablespoons parsley
½ garlic clove
½ teaspoon thyme
1 can (10½ ounces) condensed beef broth

6 small potatoes, peeled, and halved
12 small white onions, peeled
3 carrots, sliced lengthwise
1 can (4 ounces) mushroom stems and pieces, finely chopped

Cook bacon until crisp. Drain on paper towels. Reserve drippings. Cut beef into cubes. Shake a few cubes at a time in paper bag containing flour and salt. Brown cubes on all sides in bacon drippings. Remove to 2-quart casserole. Pour wine into electric blender. Add parsley, garlic, thyme, and beef broth; blend until solid ingredients are pureed. Pour over meat in casserole. Cover casserole; bake at 350 degrees for 1 hour. Stir potatoes, onions, and carrots into casserole. Replace cover. Bake 1 hour longer or until vegetables are done. Stir in mushrooms. Crumble bacon; sprinkle on top with additional chopped parsley. Makes 6 servings. *1 serving contains 15 grams carbohydrate.*

HAM HOT DISH

4 slices bread
1½ cups ham, diced,
    cooked
¾ cup diced nippy cheese
enough butter to spread
    bread

3 eggs
1½ cups milk
1 teaspoon prepared
    mustard

Cream butter and mustard. Spread on bread. Then cut
into cubes. Place in baking dish. Add ham and cheese.
Beat eggs, add milk, and pour over bread, cheese, and ham.
Bake uncovered 1 hour at 350 degrees. Serves 6. *1 serving
contains 15 grams carbohydrate.*

GLORIFIED HAMBURGER

2 pounds ground beef
1 cup onion, chopped
2 teaspoons chili powder

½ cup prepared mustard
¾ cup chili sauce
2 teaspoons salt

Brown meat and onions in fat. Add seasonings and cook
½ hour. Carbohydrate does not need to be considered.

DINNER CASSEROLE

salt and pepper to taste
1½ cups potatoes, raw,
    sliced
2 cups celery, chopped
1⅓ pounds ground beef

1 cup onions, raw, sliced
1 cup green pepper,
    chopped
2 cups tomatoes, cooked

Place layers of vegetables and meat, in order given, in
greased, shallow, baking dish. Season each layer with salt
and pepper. An additional vegetable or two will lend variety to this recipe. Bake at 350 degrees for 2 hours. 6 servings. *1 serving contains 16 grams carbohydrate.*

"LEFTOVER" SOUFFLÉ

2 tablespoons margarine
    or butter
2½ tablespoons flour
¼ teaspoon salt
⅛ teaspoon pepper
½ cup milk, skim

3 eggs, separated
1 cup "leftover" cooked
    meat, ground
few grains cayenne, optional
onion or garlic, optional—
    as desired

Melt margarine and blend in flour, salt, and pepper. Add milk gradually, stirring constantly. Cool. Add beaten egg yolks, meat, and additional seasonings. Fold in stiffly beaten egg whites and pour mixture into greased casserole. Bake until firm, 300 degrees for 45 minutes. 4 servings. *1 serving contains 5 grams carbohydrate.*

SPICED HAM LOAF

1 pound smoked ham,
    ground
2 pounds beef, ground
5 slices soft bread
    crumbs
2 eggs, beaten
1¼ cups milk

1½ teaspoons Sucaryl
    solution
1½ teaspoons salt
⅛ teaspoon pepper
½ teaspoon dry mustard
¼ teaspoon cinnamon
¼ teaspoon cloves
¼ teaspoon nutmeg

Combine ingredients in order given and mix well. Press firmly into a loaf pan. Bake at 350 degrees for 1½ hours. 8 servings. *1 serving contains 11 grams carbohydrate.*

HAM WITH CAULIFLOWER

1 head (3 cups) cauli-
    flower, separated
    into flowerettes
1 can cream of celery soup

½ cup skim milk
8 ounces ham, cooked,
    diced
1 slice bread crumbs

Cook cauliflowerettes in boiling salted water (1 inch depth) for 8 minutes. Drain. Blend soup and milk together. Mix cauliflower and ham in a greased baking dish and pour soup mixture over top. Sprinkle with bread crumbs. Bake at 350 degrees for 30 minutes. 3 servings. *1 serving contains 21 grams carbohydrate.*

HAM 'N SWEETS

½ cup skim milk
1 teaspoon Sucaryl solution (optional)
¼ teaspoon salt
⅛ teaspoon cinnamon
⅛ teaspoon nutmeg

1¼ cups sweet potatoes, boiled and mashed
1 pound ham, boiled, cut for 5 servings
2½ cups pineapple, cubed, canned unsweetened
pineapple juice to taste

Add milk, Sucaryl solution, salt, cinnamon, and nutmeg to sweet potatoes. Place ham slices in baking dish and pile potato mixture on each. Garnish with pineapple cubes and pour juice over each mound. Bake at 450 degrees for 15 minutes. 5 servings. *1 serving contains 26 grams carbohydrate.*

BARBECUED SPARERIBS

3 or 4 pounds spareribs
2 onions, sliced
2 tablespoons vinegar
2 tablespoons Worcestershire sauce

1 8-ounce bottle (¾ cup) catsup
1 teaspoon salt
¾ teaspoon paprika
¾ teaspoon chili powder
1½ cups water

Select meaty spareribs, sprinkle with salt and pepper. Place in roaster and cover with sliced onions. Pour over this the barbecue sauce. Cover and bake in 325 degree oven for 2 hours, basting occasionally. Remove cover during last 15 minutes to brown. Carbohydrate does not need to be considered.

BARBECUED BEEF SHORT RIBS

3 pounds beef short ribs
¼ teaspoon pepper
2 tablespoons lard or
   drippings
1 tablespoon Worcester-
   shire sauce
1 tablespoon flour
1 tablespoon prepared
   mustard

½ cup juice from peach,
   apple, or sweet
   pickles
2 tablespoons chopped
   onion
½ teaspoon salt
½ cup catsup

Brown short ribs in hot lard or drippings. Combine flour and mustard; add remaining ingredients and pour over short ribs. Cover and simmer 2½ hours or until tender. 6 to 8 servings. Carbohydrate does not need to be considered.

MEAT STEW

1 teaspoon fat
½ cup mixed vegetables
   (carrots, peas,
   onions)
2 or 3 ounces meat, cubed

1 small potato
Salt and pepper to taste
1 cup water
celery leaves

Brown meat in fat. Add water, salt, pepper and a few celery leaves for seasoning. Simmer slowly until meat is tender. Add vegetables. Cut potato into quarters and add. Cook for 30 minutes or until vegetables are done. *1 serving contains 22 grams carbohydrate.*

CREAMED CHIPPED BEEF

4 ounces dried beef
3 tablespoons margarine
3 tablespoons flour
1½ cups milk, skim,
   scalded

1 egg
¾ slice toast quarters
3 pimiento olives
few sprigs parsley
sprinkling paprika

Pull beef apart into small pieces. Cover with hot water. Let stand several minutes and then drain. Melt shortening and blend in flour to make a smooth paste. Add scalded milk slowly and cook over hot water until thick. Add beef and heat thoroughly. Just before removing from heat add slightly-beaten egg. Serve on toast quarters garnished with sliced olives, parsley, and a sprinkling of paprika. 3 servings. *1 serving contains 15 grams carbohydrate.*

BEEF PORCUPINES

1 pound lean ground beef
¼ cup uncooked rice
1 egg slightly beaten
½ cup minced onion
2 tablespoons minced parsley
1 teaspoon salt

10½ ounce can condensed tomato soup
½ tablespoon vegetable oil
1 small clove garlic, minced
1 cup water

Mix first 6 ingredients with ¼ cup condensed soup and form into about 15 1½″ balls. Brown meat balls and garlic in vegetable oil in skillet. Then blend in remaining soup and 1 cup water. Cover and simmer about 40 minutes, until rice is tender. Makes 5 servings. *1 serving contains 15 grams carbohydrate.*

BEEF STROGANOFF

½ cup braised fat-free beef cubes
1 teaspoon chopped onion
1 teaspoon chopped green pepper
¼ teaspoon garlic salt
¼ teaspoon salt
dash pepper
2 tablespoons mushroom liquid or water

¼ cup cream of mushroom soup, condensed
2 tablespoons sliced mushrooms
¼ cup strained buttermilk
1 teaspoon Worcestershire sauce
2 teaspoons flour, to thicken

Simmer beef, onions, green pepper, and mushroom juice or water until meat is tender and vegetables are slightly cooked. Add mushroom soup, sliced mushrooms, buttermilk, and Worcestershire sauce and bring to a boil. Make a paste of flour and a little water, and stir into the simmering beef mixture. Serves 8. *1 serving contains 7 grams carbohydrate.*

MEAT LOAF

1 pound ground lean meat
⅓ cup soft bread crumbs
3 tablespoons finely cut onions
⅓ cup drained, canned tomatoes
salt and pepper to taste

Mix ingredients thoroughly. Shape into loaf and place into greased shallow baking pan. Bake in oven at 350° for 40 minutes or until brown. 4 servings. Carbohydrate does not need to be considered.

SAUTÉED LIVER

1 slice liver, ½ inch thick
flour
salt and pepper

Remove outer membrane and veins from liver and wipe with a damp cloth. Dredge with flour, salt, and pepper and cook in a well-greased pan for 6 to 7 minutes, turning frequently. Liver may be served with strips of bacon or with sautéed onions. Calves' liver is very tender, but beef, lamb, or pig liver is equally nutritious and much less expensive.

BACON

Arrange bacon in a cold frying pan and cook over moderate flame until edges begin to curl. If the bacon has just been removed from the refrigerator, the strips may be separated as the bacon cooks. Turn each slice separately, and remove before fat of bacon looks dry. Pour off the fat as it accumulates. Place in pan lined with absorbent paper to drain. Properly cooked bacon is crisp and readily broken with a fork; if underdone, it will be tough and have to be cut with a knife. Carbohydrate does not need to be considered.

VEAL WITH NOODLES

18 ounces veal, cooked, cubed (about 3 cups)	¾ cup uncooked noodles
2 cups celery, chopped	1½ teaspoons salt
½ cup green pepper, chopped	⅛ teaspoon pepper
	2½ cups tomato juice

Place all ingredients in a casserole and mix well. Cover and bake at 300 degrees for 2 hours. 6 servings. *1 serving contains 7 grams carbohydrate.*

VEAL AND ONIONS

2 large onions, sliced	1 pound veal cutlet
3 tablespoons margarine	2 teaspoons paprika
5 tablespoons flour	1¼ cups milk

Sauté onion in shortening. Mix flour with salt. Cut veal into strips, roll in flour mixture, add to onions, and brown. Sprinkle with paprika and add milk gradually. Simmer 20 to 30 minutes. 4 servings. *1 serving contains 5 grams carbohydrate.*

BLANQUETTE DE VEAU

2 pounds veal	1 tablespoon flour
1 tablespoon butter	2 teaspoons butter
2 onions	2 egg yolks
2 carrots	1 teaspoon vinegar
parsley, thyme, bayleaf salt, pepper	1 teaspoon butter

Have breast of veal cut into small pieces. Place in a casserole with the butter, carrots, salt, pepper, and the parsley, thyme, and a bayleaf tied together. Pour in water until the meat is nearly covered and let simmer for 2 hours in the casserole which should be tightly closed. Before serving, pour off 2 cups of the bouillon, and add to the mixture of butter and flour which you have prepared in a saucepan. Let this sauce mixture reduce by about one-third and add egg yolks, vinegar, and butter. When thick, add mushrooms which have been sliced and browned in butter for 10 minutes, and pour over the meat from which you have removed the vegetables. Carbohydrate does not need to be considered.

LAMB KABOBS

1 small clove garlic
½ cup salad oil
¼ cup vinegar
1 teaspoon dry mustard
dash of cayenne, mushroom
    caps

8 to 10 long metal skewers
2 pound lamb shoulder,
    cut in 1-inch cubes
1 teaspoon Worcestershire
    sauce

Rub bowl with garlic, place lamb cubes in it. Mix oil, vinegar, and seasonings and marinate lamb in this anywhere from 4 to 12 hours in refrigerator. Drain. Thread lamb on skewers alternating with mushrooms. In broiler preheated 8 minutes, cook kabobs 10 to 20 minutes turning till browned on all sides. Serves 6. Carbohydrate does not need to be considered.

LAMB LOAF

2 pounds ground lamb	½ cup green pepper, chopped
1 egg	
1 cup milk, skim	1½ teaspoons salt
1 cup cracker crumbs	dash of pepper
2 tablespoons parsley, chopped	1¼ cups apricot puree (optional)
2 tablespoons onion, minced	

Mix all ingredients, except apricot puree, thoroughly and pack into a ring mold. Bake at 300 degrees for 1 hour. Spread apricot puree over top of the loaf and return to the oven. Bake for remaining half hour. 9 servings. *1 serving contains 18 grams carbohydrate. 1 serving without apricot puree contains 9 grams carbohydrate.*

VEAL-RICE HOT DISH

VEAL

1 pound veal, cut in small cubes	1 cup celery, chopped fine
1 large onion, chopped fine	¼ pound butter

Brown veal thoroughly in butter over medium heat. Add onion and celery and simmer until partially cooked.

RICE

1 small can mushroom soup	1 cup water
1 small can chicken soup	½ cup rice (scant)

Heat soup and water to boiling, add rice and let stand—not cook—until meat mixture is ready. Combine, season well, put in baking dish. Bake 1½ hours at 375°. One half

hour before removing from oven, sprinkle with 15¢ worth
of salted almonds chopped fine. Six portions. *½ cup rice
contains 15 grams carbohydrate.*

BROILED CHICKEN

Dip a leg and thigh section or the breast and wing portion of chicken in small amount of milk. Sprinkle with suggested Seasonings*. Place in baking pan or on foil. Bake
in oven at 350 degrees for 1 hour.

Seasoning*: In a shaker container, combine salt, pepper, paprika, finely powdered parsley and a very small
amount of oregano and marjoram.

Variation: After dipping chicken in milk, roll in crumbled cornflakes, or dried bread crumbs. (3 tablespoons or
¾ cup cornflake crumbs, equals 15 grams carbohydrate)
1 serving chicken contains 15 grams carbohydrate.

CHICKEN CHOW MEIN, AMERICAN STYLE

1 tablespoon butter or margarine
4 tablespoons minced onion
1½ cups shredded cooked chicken
1 cup celery, diced
1½ cups meat stock or water
2 tablespoons soy sauce
1½ tablespoons cornstarch
3 tablespoons cold water
Chow Mein noodles

Brown onion lightly in margarine. Add next 4 ingredients and simmer 15 minutes. Blend and stir into meat mixture, cornstarch mixed in cold water. Cook until slightly
thickened and clear. Serve hot on Chow Mein noodles.
Serves 4. *½ cup Chow Mein noodles contains 15 grams
carbohydrate.*

CHICKEN CACCIATORE

2½ to 3 pound broiler
1 clove garlic
1 cup chopped onion
1 medium green pepper, seeded and sliced into strips
1 chicken bouillon cube
2 tablespoons oil

1 cup boiling water
1-pound can tomatoes
8-ounce can tomato sauce
1 tablespoon salt
½ teaspoon pepper
dash cayenne pepper
¼ teaspoon marjoram
2 bay leaves

Season chicken with salt and pepper. Brown chicken in broiler on both sides. In skillet sauté onions, garlic, and green pepper in oil. Add seasonings, tomatoes and tomato sauce, bouillon, and water. Heat to boiling. Add chicken, cover, and simmer 1 hour, basting from time to time. Remove cover during last half-hour. 3-ounce portions or as desired. Carbohydrate does not need to be considered.

OVEN BARBECUED CHICKEN

1 frying chicken cut into serving pieces
¼ cut water
¾ cup vinegar
3 tablespoon salad oil
¼ cup catsup or chili sauce

1 teaspoon dry mustard
1½ teaspoons salt
½ teaspoon pepper
2 tablespoons chopped onion

Preheat oven to 350 degrees. Combine all ingredients except chicken in saucepan, place over heat, and simmer for 5 to 10 minutes. Place chicken, skin side up, in large baking pan. Pour half of the barbecue sauce over chicken and bake, uncovered, for about 60 minutes. Baste with remaining barbecue sauce every 15 minutes. Roast till tender. Carbohydrate does not need to be considered.

BAKED CHICKEN AND RICE

½ cup rice, cooked
½ cup diced chicken
¼ cup clear broth
salt and pepper to taste

chopped parsley, onions,
celery, mushrooms,
green pepper, pi-
miento, or tomatoes
may be added if
desired

Combine the above ingredients and place in small casserole. Bake in moderate oven (350 degrees) until brown.
Noodles or spaghetti may be used in place of rice. For the
chicken, any type of meat or fish may be used. *1 serving
contains 15 grams carbohydrate.*

CHICKEN LOAF

3 cups chicken, cooked,
   cut in pieces
½ cup chicken broth,
   without fat
3 slices bread, crumbed
½ cup rice, cooked
1½ teaspoons salt

¼ teaspoon pepper
½ cup milk
1 tablespoon onion,
   minced
1 tablespoon green pep-
   per, chopped
1 egg

Heat chicken broth and add chicken, crumbs, rice, salt,
pepper, milk, onion, green pepper, and beaten egg. Press
firmly into greased loaf pan and bake in 325 degree oven
for 1 hour. If gravy is desired, use 3 tablespoons flour with
2 cups of chicken broth. This will not add appreciably to
the carbohydrate value of one serving. 6 servings. *1 serving
contains 11 grams carbohydrate.*

CREAMED CHICKEN ON TOAST

½ cup margarine or butter
½ cup flour
3 cups milk
2 tablespoons parsley, minced
1 teaspoon salt
2 teaspoons onion, grated
1 teaspoon Worcestershire sauce
few grains cayenne
3 cups chicken, cut in pieces, cooked
1 cup mushroom sliced, cooked
8 slices bread for toast

Melt margarine in top of a double boiler. Blend in flour and gradually add milk, stirring constantly. Cook until thick. Add remaining ingredients and serve on the toast. 8 servings. *1 serving contains 25 grams carbohydrate.*

SCALLOPED CHICKEN

3 cups chicken, cooked
1½ cups chicken broth
3 cups cooked rice
4 tablespoons margarine
3 tablespoons flour
2 teaspoons salt
dash pepper
1 cup skim milk, scalded
2 cups mushrooms, sliced
3 slices bread, crumbed
⅓ cup blanched almonds, shredded
1 small jar pimiento, cut in pieces
sprinkling paprika

Pour 1 cup of the chicken broth over rice. To make the gravy, melt 2 tablespoons margarine in top of double boiler and blend in flour, salt, pepper. Add remaining ½ cup chicken broth and the milk. Cook until thick, stirring constantly. Remove from heat and cover. Brown mushrooms in 1 tablespoon margarine. Brown crumbs in 1 tablespoon margarine, very lightly. Cover bottom of casserole with rice. Place layer of chicken over rice, cover with gravy. Dot with almonds and pimiento. Add layer of mushrooms and top with buttered crumbs. Sprinkle with paprika. Bake in 325 degree oven for 30 minutes. This recipe may be prepared a day or two in advance and kept in refrigerator until ready to bake and serve. 6 servings. *1 serving contains 36 grams carbohydrate.*

FRIED CHICKEN

2 to 3 pounds chicken   **salt and pepper to taste**
flour   **fat for frying**

Have chicken cut in attractive pieces. Wash chicken and wipe with damp cloth. Roll chicken in flour to which salt and pepper have been added. Heat fat ½ inch deep in a skillet. Add pieces of chicken, turning as necessary with a pair of tongs until brown. Cover and cook slowly until tender. Uncover during the last 5 or 10 minutes of cooking to recrisp the skin. Carbohydrate does not need to be considered.

TURKEY DIVAN

1 package frozen broccoli   **4 slices hot toast**
   spears, cooked   **Mornay Sauce (p. 47)**
8 slices cooked turkey,
   white meat

In advance prepare Mornay Sauce, cook broccoli, and cut turkey in thick slices. Preheat oven to 400 degrees. Place 4 slices of toast on a 12″ x 9″ dish. Next place a layer of cooked turkey slices. Partially cook and lay on top of meat, 1 package frozen broccoli or asparagus, well drained. Cover with Mornay Sauce. Heat in oven until the sauce is browned and bubbling. Serves 4. *1 serving contains 15 grams carbohydrate.*

HAM-TURKEY PIE

4 tablespoons butter or margarine	1 cup diced cooked turkey
5 tablespoons all-purpose flour	½ cup sliced mushrooms
¼ teaspoon pepper	¼ cup chopped green onion
2 cups chicken broth	3 tablespoons snipped parsley
1 cup diced cooked ham	1 Rice Shell

In saucepan, melt margarine; blend in flour and pepper. Add chicken broth all at once. Cook over medium heat, stirring constantly, till mixture thickens and bubbles. Add ham, turkey, mushrooms, onion, parsley; mix thoroughly. Pour into prepared Rice Shell. Bake in 350 degree oven for 40 minutes. Let stand 5 to 8 minutes. 6 servings. *1 serving contains 22 grams carbohydrate.*

Rice Shell: Combine 2½ cups cooked long-grain rice, 2 beaten eggs, 4 tablespoons melted margarine, and ⅛ teaspoon pepper; mix thoroughly. Press firmly into an ungreased 9-inch pie plate.

TURKEY CURRY

1 can (4 ounces) drained mushrooms	½ cup grated or finely chopped fresh coconut
¼ cup margarine or butter	1 teaspoon curry powder or more if desired
¼ cup flour	½ teaspoon ginger
1 teaspoon salt	¼ teaspoon celery seed
1½ cups liquid broth	¼ teaspoon white pepper
½ cup cream	4 cups cooked rice (1½ cups raw rice)
2 to 3 cups diced turkey	

Brown mushrooms in the butter or margarine. Add flour and salt and cook until bubbly. Pour in liquid, including cream, all at once. Continue cooking, stirring constantly until uniformly thickened. Add turkey, coconut and seasonings. Cook 10 to 15 minutes longer over simmering water in a double boiler or over low heat. Stir occasionally to keep from sticking to pan. Serve over hot rice, 8 servings. *½ cup rice contains 15 grams carbohydrate.* (Veal or chicken are good substitutes for turkey.)

TURKEY BURGERS

2 cups chopped cooked turkey
1 egg, slightly beaten
½ cup mayonnaise
½ cup diced celery
¼ cup fine dry flavored or plain bread crumbs
2 tablespoons finely chopped onion
2 tablespoons finely chopped blanched almonds
¼ teaspoon salt
¼ teaspoon pepper
bread crumbs
1 tablespoon margarine
3 English muffins, split and toasted
lettuce

Mix together first 9 ingredients. Chill for 1 hour. Shape into 6 patties; roll in bread crumbs. Melt margarine in skillet over medium heat. Cook about 10 minutes or until evenly browned. Serve on muffin halves with lettuce. 6 servings. *1 serving contains 15 grams carbohydrate.*

PHEASANT SUPREME

3 to 4 pounds pheasant (2 birds)
¼ cup salad oil
1 cup diced celery
2 tablespoons minced onion
salt and pepper to taste
flour
¼ cup sherry
¾ cup light cream

Cut up pheasant, season, flour lightly, and fry slowly in oil. Transfer to casserole. Add celery, onion, and 1 tablespoon flour to oil in frying pan. Stir over low heat 2 minutes and add to pheasant. Add sherry and cream, cover, and bake in 350 degree oven for 1 hour or until tender. Chicken may be used. Carbohydrate does not need to be considered.

Fish

OVEN-BROILED FISH

Wipe fish with a cloth after washing thoroughly. Dot with margarine or butter, season with salt and pepper, and place skin side down on a greased broiler rack. Cook for 8 to 12 minutes or until fish is brown and flakes when touched with a pointed knife. Serve with parsley butter sauce or tartar sauce. No carbohydrate to be considered.

PAN-FRIED FISH

Wash fish, and wipe dry with cloth. Melt 1 tablespoon of butter or margarine in a frying pan. Dip fish in flour, season with salt and pepper, and sauté until brown on both sides. Carbohydrate does not need to be considered.

OVEN-BAKED FISH

Wash fish and wipe dry with a cloth. Place skin side down in baking pan. Dot with margarine or butter. Season with salt, pepper, paprika, and parsley. Place in 400 degree oven for 25 minutes. Turn fish over once during the baking period. Serve with lemon wedges. May add a little white wine while baking if desired. Carbohydrate does not need to be considered.

FISH SKILLET

1 pound fish fillets or steaks
3 tablespoons salad oil
1 onion, chopped
3 tablespoons chopped green pepper
2 tablespoons chopped parsley
2 medium tomatoes, cut in pieces or 1 8-ounce can stewed tomatoes
½ cup water or tomato juice
½ teaspoon salt
½ teaspoon basil or oregano
dash pepper

Frozen fish should be thawed to separate pieces. Heat oil in skillet, add onion, green pepper, and parsley. Cook until onion is golden. Add tomatoes, water or tomato juice, and seasoning. Cook until tomatoes are soft. Add fish. Cover and cook gently about 10 minutes, or until fish is done. 4 servings. Carbohydrate does not need to be considered.

SALMON CAKES

2 ounces canned salmon
½ cup mashed potatoes
¼ teaspoon salt
pepper to taste
½ teaspoon grated onion
5 small stuffed olives, sliced
2 teaspoons margarine or butter

Combine all ingredients, except margarine. Shape into 2 cakes. Brown in margarine. Serve hot. *1 cake contains 7 grams carbohydrate.*

SALMON SOUFFLÉ

½ cup milk
1 slice bread, crumbed
1 cup salmon
2 teaspoons lemon juice

3 eggs, separated
¼ teaspoon salt
⅛ teaspoon paprika
Tabasco to taste

Heat milk and crumbs in top of double boiler. Flake salmon, mix with lemon juice, and add to hot mixture. Add well-beaten egg yolks and cook until thick. Season with salt, paprika, and Tabasco sauce. Fold in stiffly-beaten egg whites, and turn into buttered casserole. Set in pan of hot water and bake until firm. 300 degrees oven 1 hour. 4 servings. *1 serving contains 5 grams carbohydrate.*

SHRIMP CREOLE

12 ounces raw shrimp
½ cup minced onion
2 tablespoons salad oil
1-pound can tomatoes
1 clove garlic, minced
1 8-ounce can tomato
    sauce
1½ teaspoons salt

½ to 1 teaspoon chili
    powder
1 tablespoon Worcester-
    shire sauce
dash of bottled hot pepper
    sauce
2 teaspoons cornstarch
½ cup chopped green
    pepper

Sauté onion in salad oil. Add remaining ingredients, except shrimp. Let simmer for 20 minutes. Add shrimp. Simmer for 10 minutes more. 6 servings. Carbohydrate does not need to be considered.

CRABMEAT CASSEROLE

2 cups cooked rice
1 cup grated, sharp cheese
2 tablespoons chopped
  onion
3 beaten egg yolks
1 6½-ounce can crabmeat

¼ cup margarine or butter,
  melted
salt and pepper to taste
1 cup chopped parsley
3 egg whites, beaten stiff

Combine all ingredients except egg whites, blend thoroughly. Fold in egg whites. Bake in greased baking dish in moderate oven for 25 minutes. Serve with a sauce made of 1 can of condensed mushroom soup diluted with ½ cup of water, heated just to the simmering point but not boiled. 6 serving. *1 serving contains 10 grams of carbohydrate.*

DEVILED TUNA OR CRAB

2 tablespoons butter or
  margarine
1 tablespoon minced
  onion
2 tablespoons flour
½ teaspoon salt
¼ teaspoon dry mustard
1 cup skim milk
1 teaspoon Worcestershire
  sauce
dash Tabasco sauce
2 teaspoons lemon juice
½ cup celery, chopped

¼ cup pimiento, chopped
1 tablespoon parsley,
  chopped
½ cup green pepper,
  chopped
2 hard boiled eggs,
  chopped
¼ teaspoon paprika
2 cans tuna or crabmeat
  (8½-ounce can)
2 slices bread, soft crumbs
1 tablespoon margarine

Melt margarine and add minced onion. Cook for about 1 minute over low heat. Add flour, salt, mustard. Add milk gradually, stirring constantly until mixture thickens. Add remaining ingredients, except for bread crumbs and margarine. Pour into a greased baking dish and top with crumbs that have been mixed with melted margarine. Bake in 350 degree oven for 20 minutes. 6 servings. *1 serving contains 11 grams carbohydrate.*

TOMATO-TUNA RABBITS

4 slices toast	¼ teaspoon salt
4 teaspoons margarine	¼ teaspoon dry mustard
1 can tuna fish (8 ounces)	½ cup skim milk, scalded
4 tomato slices, thick	¼ pound cheese, sharp,
sprinkling salt	grated
1 tablespoon margarine	2 tablespoons green pep-
1 tablespoon flour	per, chopped

Spread each slice of toast with ½ teaspoon margarine. Cover with tuna flakes, place slice of tomato on top of each, dot each with ½ teaspoon margarine, and sprinkle with salt. Bake at 425 degrees for 10 minutes. Make cheese sauce as follows: Melt 1 tablespoon margarine in top of double boiler. Blend in flour, salt, and mustard. Add milk gradually and stir until thick. Add grated cheese and green pepper, cook over low heat until cheese is melted. Pour sauce over baked combination. Serve at once. 4 servings. *1 serving contains 16 grams carbohydrate.*

SHRIMP DELIGHT

1 pound fresh or frozen	½ teaspoon pickling spice
shrimp	1 tablespoon vinegar
3 cups boiling water	½ stick margarine
1 teaspoon salt	1 teaspoon Worcestershire
1 bay leaf	sauce
3 celery tops and leaves	

Add shrimp, seasonings, and vinegar to boiling water. Cook about 15 minutes, then drain, peel, and clean shrimp. Put margarine in skillet, melt, and add Worcester-shire sauce, heat shrimp in this until heated through, about 5 minutes. 4 servings. Carbohydrate does not need to be considered.

CASSEROLE OF BAKED CRAB IMPERIAL

4 tablespoons margarine or butter	1 egg yolk, beaten
4 tablespoons flour	2 tablespoons sherry
2 cups milk	1 cup soft bread crumbs
1 teaspoon salt	1 pound crab flakes
⅛ teaspoon pepper	1 teaspoon minced parsley
½ teaspoon celery salt	1 teaspoon minced onion
dash of cayenne	¼ cup buttered crumbs
	paprika

Melt margarine, add flour, and blend. Gradually add milk and seasonings. Cook over low heat until thickened. Gradually add egg yolk and cook 2 minutes more. Remove from heat and add sherry, bread crumbs, crab meat, parsley, and onion. Gently mix, then pour into well-greased 1½-quart casserole. Top with buttered crumbs and sprinkle with paprika. Bake in 350 degree oven for 20 to 25 minutes. Serves 8. *1 serving contains 15 grams carbohydrate.*

CRAB NEWBURG

2 tablespoons flour	⅛ teaspoon red pepper
½ teaspoon salt	1 teaspoon Worcestershire sauce
3 tablespoons margarine or butter, melted	2 cans crab meat (8 ounce cans)
1½ cups milk	
2 egg yolks, beaten	2 slices toast
½ teaspoon paprika	

Blend flour and salt with melted margarine in top of double boiler. Add milk and egg yolks which have been beaten together. Cook over hot water until thick. Add seasonings and crab meat and cook three minutes. Serve on toast. 4 servings. *1 serving contains 15 grams carbohydrate.*

Noodles, Cheese, Eggs

ITALIAN DINNER

¼ cup salad oil	3 cups spaghetti, cooked
1 pound ground steak (round)	1 cup mushrooms, canned
2 tablespoons onion, grated	⅔ cup corn, cooked
½ cup green pepper, chopped	1 can tomato sauce
	1 tablespoon Worcestershire sauce

Heat oil and mix well with the ground steak, grated onion, and chopped pepper. Add spaghetti, mushrooms, corn, tomato sauce, and Worcestershire sauce. Place in baking dish. Bake at 350 degrees for 45 minutes. 8 servings. *1 serving contains 24 grams carbohydrate.*

LASAGNA CASSEROLE

1 pound lean ground beef
½ cup onion, chopped
6-ounce can tomato paste
2-pound can of tomatoes
2 teaspoons salt
½ teaspoon oregano

½ pound Cheddar cheese, shredded
¼ cup Parmesan cheese
8-ounce package lasagna noodles
1 teaspoon salad oil
½ cup thinly sliced celery

Lightly coat large, heavy skillet with a little oil. Heat the skillet to medium hot. Add ground beef; mash and stir to break up particles; add chopped onion, thinly sliced celery, tomatoes, seasonings, tomato paste. Cover and simmer 20 minutes. Heat oven to 350 degrees. In oblong baking dish, 11½" x 7" x 1½" alternate layers of cooked noodles, Cheddar cheese, Parmesan cheese and of meat sauce. Bake 45 minutes at 350 degrees. 6 servings. *1/6 of casserole is 37 grams carbohydrate.*

SPAGHETTI SAUCE WITH MEAT

1 pound ground beef
1 8-ounce can tomato sauce
1-pound can tomatoes
2 tablespoons green pepper
1 teaspoon mustard

dash of oregano
¾ cup water
½ cup onion, chopped
¼ cup celery, chopped
salt and pepper to taste
1 tablespoon Worcestershire sauce

In skillet break up ground hamburger and brown. Drain off fat. Add all other ingredients. Bring to boil, reduce heat, and simmer for 1 hour, 15 minutes. Serve over spaghetti. 1 cup of sauce does not need to be considered for carbohydrate. *½ cup cooked spaghetti contains 15 grams carbohydrate.*

ITALIAN SPAGHETTI

½ cup cooked spaghetti
1 teaspoon fat, butter or
   margarine
½ small onion, chopped
2 ounces ground meat

2 tablespoons tomato
   paste
¼ cup water
salt and pepper to taste
½ cup tomatoes

Brown the onion and ground meat in the fat, drain off the fat. Add the tomato paste, water, tomatoes, and seasonings. Allow to simmer gently 1 hour or more. If needed, add more water. Serve on ½ cup spaghetti. Sprinkle 2 teaspoons grated cheese on top. *1 serving contains 15 grams carbohydrate.*

MACARONI AND CHEESE

¼ cup broth
½ cup diced cheese
½ cup macaroni, cooked

salt, pepper, dash of
   mustard

Cook cheese and broth together in double boiler until smooth. Add macaroni and mix well. Bake in 350 degree oven about 20 minutes or until brown. In place of macaroni, ½ cup cooked rice, noodles, or spaghetti may be used. *1 serving contains 15 grams carbohydrate.*

NOODLE BAKE

2 cups Cheddar cheese,
   cubed
¼ cup milk

½ cup cooked or drained
   canned green beans
½ cup cooked noodles
salt, pepper, paprika

Melt cheese in milk in small saucepan over low heat; blend until smooth. Combine with beans, noodles, salt, and pepper. Place in individual casserole; sprinkle with paprika. Bake in 350 degree oven for 20 minutes or until brown. *1 serving contains 18 grams carbohydrate.*

MACARONI AND CHEESE SQUARES

1½ cups skim milk, scalded	½ pound American cheese, grated
3 slices bread, soft, cubed	½ teaspoon salt
2 tablespoons margarine or butter	⅛ teaspoon pepper
	3 eggs, beaten
¼ cup pimiento, chopped	1 cup macaroni, cooked
1½ tablespoons onion, minced	½ teaspoon paprika
	few sprigs parsley

Pour milk over bread cubes. Add margarine, pimiento, onion, cheese, and seasonings. Mix well. Add beaten eggs and macaroni. Pour into a greased baking dish, 8" x 12". Sprinkle with paprika. Bake at 325 degrees for 50 minutes. Cut in squares. Serve with mushrooms or mushroom sauce, if desired. Add sprigs of parsley. 6 servings. *1 serving contains 15 grams carbohydrate.*

MACARONI HOT DISH

2 cups warm cooked macaroni	2 tablespoons melted margarine
1½ cups grated cheese	pepper and salt to taste
1½ cups bread crumbs	1½ cups milk
1 green pepper, diced	1 can Campbell's Mushroom Soup
3 eggs, beaten	
1 onion, diced	

Mix all ingredients except mushroom soup. Put in pan set in hot water. Cut in squares and pour over it undiluted mushroom soup which has been heated. 6 servings. *1 serving contains 30 grams carbohydrate.*

CHEESE FONDUE

1 egg	salt, pepper, chopped
1 cup chicken broth	parsley, onion grated
1 slice bread, cubed	(1 small)
¼ cup cheese, diced	

Beat the egg, add broth, bread, cheese and seasonings. Bake in a moderate oven, 350 degrees, until firm in the center, about 20 to 30 minutes. In place of cheese, ¼ cup chopped ham, chicken, tuna fish, or salmon may be used. *1 serving contains 15 grams carbohydrate.*

CHEESE SOUFFLÉ

1 tablespoon shortening, either butter or margarine	⅔ cup chicken broth
2 tablespoons flour	⅔ cup grated American cheese or 2 ounces diced processed variety
½ teaspoon salt	
few grains pepper	2 eggs, separated

Melt margarine, stir in flour, salt, and pepper. Stir in broth and cook over low heat until mixture thickens. Add grated cheese and stir until melted. Stir into lightly beaten egg yolks. Fold in stiffly beaten egg whites. Pour into a quart, ungreased baking dish or individual ramekins. Set into pan of hot water. Bake in slow oven, 325 degrees, for 1 hour or until knife, when inserted in center, comes out clean. Serve at once. 4 servings. Carbohydrate does not need to be considered.

WELSH RABBIT

1 tablespoon margarine	2 teaspoons Worcestershire sauce
½ pound American cheese, diced	½ cup milk, skim
½ teaspoon salt	1 egg
½ teaspoon dry mustard	6 slices toast
½ teaspoon Tabasco sauce	

Melt margarine over low heat. Stir in and melt cheese. Add salt, mustard, Tabasco sauce, Worcestershire sauce and gradually milk. Remove from fire and add a little of the cheese mixture to beaten egg. Return to pan and mix thoroughly. Serve over the hot toast. 6 servings. *1 serving contains 16 grams carbohydrate.*

CHILI CON CARNE

1 pound ground lean beef	1 8-ounce can tomato sauce
1 cup onion, chopped	1 teaspoon salt
1-pound can of kidney beans	2 teaspoons chili powder
	1 bay leaf

Stir and sauté ground beef and onions together until beef is well done. Add kidney beans, tomato sauce, salt, chili powder, and bay leaf. Cover and cook slowly for 1 hour. Makes 5 servings. *1 serving contains 15 grams carbohydrate.*

WELSH RAREBIT

2 cups shredded sharp process American cheese	1 teaspoon dry mustard
	dash of cayenne
¾ cup milk	1 egg, well beaten
1 teaspoon Worcestershire sauce	sliced tomatoes
	4 slices toast

In heavy saucepan, heat cheese and milk over very low heat, stirring constantly until cheese melts and sauce is smooth. Add next three ingredients. Stir in small amount of the hot mixture in beaten egg, then add to the hot mixture. Cook and stir over very low heat until mixture thickens and is creamy. Serve at once over hot toast with sliced tomatoes. 4 servings. *1 serving contains 16 grams carbohydrate.*

SCRAMBLED EGGS

4 eggs   ¼ teaspoon salt
¼ cup water   few grains pepper

Beat eggs slightly in top of double boiler. Stir in water, salt, and pepper. Cook over boiling water, stirring constantly until eggs are firm. You may also cook the eggs in a fry pan after melting margarine and then pouring in the eggs and stirring with a fork till scrambled to your liking. The addition of grated cheese gives variety, as does the addition of crumbled bacon. 4 servings. Carbohydrate does not need to be considered.

SPANISH OMELET

1 egg   ½ teaspoon chopped
1½ teaspoons water   green pepper
½ teaspoon chopped   salt and pepper to taste
    onion   1 teaspoon butter or
                         margarine

Break egg and beat until yellow and thick. Add water, onion, green pepper, salt and pepper. Melt margarine in small frying pan and pour in mixture. Cook slowly over low flame until golden brown. 1 serving. Carbohydrate does not need to be considered.

STUFFED EGGS IN CHEESE

6 hard cooked eggs. Shell eggs, halve and remove yolk, mash yolks with:

2 tablespoons mayonnaise	½ teaspoon salt
1 teaspoon prepared mustard	pepper

Stuff eggs with mixture and place in shallow baking dish, copper or glass or individual casseroles. Cover with cheese sauce made of:

2 tablespoons margarine or butter	1 teaspoon Worcestershire sauce
2 tablespoons flour	salt and pepper
1 cup milk	3 tablespoons sherry
½ cup grated cheese	

Lay slices of fresh or canned mushrooms on top. Bake in a moderate oven until cheese bubbles. Garnish with paprika and parsley. 4 servings. *1 serving contains 6 grams carbohydrate.*

COUNTRY CLUB EGGS

½ cup chopped onions	2 tablespoons chopped parsley
2 tablespoons flour	
1½ cups milk	2 tablespoons lemon juice
salt and pepper to taste	
6 hard boiled eggs, sliced	1½ cups grated cheese
1 teaspoon minced parsley	4 slices of toast
	pimiento, minced

Cook onion in small amount of fat until soft and yellow. Add flour, stir. Add milk. Cook until thick and smooth, stirring constantly. Add salt and pepper to taste. Add parsley, lemon juice, and pimiento. Add cheese and stir until melted. Arrange eggs on buttered toast. Pour the cheese sauce over the eggs. Sprinkle with paprika. 4 servings. *1 serving contains 23 grams carbohydrate.*

Vegetables

SERVICE OF VEGETABLES

Vegetables may be served in a variety of ways: (1) Buttered: Add 1 to 2 teaspoons butter with a dash of salt and pepper to ½ cup diced and cooked vegetables. Minced parsley with potatoes or carrots, a dash of nutmeg with green beans, lemon juice with spinach, minced green pepper and pimiento with corn, mint leaves with peas suggest a few of many possibilities for enhancing flavor and interest of vegetables. (2) With cream: Add 1 tablespoon hot cream to ½ cup of hot buttered vegetables. (3) With sauces of blending or contrasting flavor: (a) pour ¼ cup hot white sauce (medium) over ½ cup cooked vegetable;

(b) cheese sauce is especially suitable for cabbage, cauliflower, asparagus; (c) hollandaise sauce lends a piquant flavor to asparagus and broccoli. (4) Escalloped: Mix ½ cup cooked vegetables with ¼ to ½ cup medium white sauce. Place in a buttered baking dish and cover with bread or cracker crumbs. Dot with butter and bake in oven until crumbs are brown.

GREEN RICE

¾ cup uncooked rice
1 package frozen spinach
   (10 ounces)
1½ cups water

3 tablespoons minced
   onion
1 tablespoon margarine
   or butter
1½ teaspoons salt

Heat oven to 350 degrees. Mix all ingredients in greased 1 or 1½ quart casserole or baking dish 10″ x 6″ x 1½″ or 11½″ x 7½″ x 1½″. Cover tightly. Bake until liquid is absorbed and rice is tender, 25 to 30 minutes. Use regular rice, not the instant or converted rice. 6 servings. *1 serving contains 22 grams carbohydrate.*

VEGETABLE MIXTURE

½ cup water
1 box frozen broccoli
   flowerettes
1 box frozen French-cut
   green beans
2 medium onions, cut into
   large strips

1 cup fresh mushrooms,
   sliced, or 4-ounce can
   sliced mushrooms
2 teaspoons butter or
   margarine
dash of garlic powder
1 teaspoon soy sauce
salt and pepper to taste

Place ingredients in saucepan. Cover. Bring to full boil. Separate gently with fork. Cover again and simmer 3 to 5 minutes. Do not overcook. Vegetables should be slightly crisp. 8 servings. Carbohydrate does not need to be considered.

BAKED POTATO

1 small size potato   1 teaspoon butter

Scrub potato with a brush; dry and slightly grease the surface. Place in a moderately hot oven (425 degrees) and bake about 45 to 50 minutes. The potato should feel tender under pressure. When done, make an incision of 1 inch in the skin and gently press the potato so that excess moisture can escape. Put butter in the cut and serve immediately. *15 grams carbohydrate.*

BAKED STUFFED POTATO

1 potato, small   salt and pepper
1 teaspoon butter   2 teaspoons grated cheese
1 tablespoon cream   paprika

Bake potato as directed above. Cut thin slice from side of potato and remove pulp from casing. Mash and mix with butter and hot cream. Season with salt and pepper, and beat until creamy. Return to potato shell and sprinkle with cheese and paprika. Place in hot oven and cook until cheese is melted and browned. *15 grams carbohydrate.*

MASHED POTATO

1 cooked small sized potato 1 tablespoon hot cream
1 teaspoon butter   salt and pepper

Mash potato until free of lumps, add butter, hot cream, and salt and pepper to taste. Beat until creamy. *15 grams carbohydrate.*

SWEET POTATO SOUFFLÉ

2 cups sweet potatoes, cooked, mashed	1 teaspoon salt pepper, as desired
¾ cup milk, skim, hot	3 egg whites, stiffly-beaten
¼ cup margarine	
1 tablespoon lemon rind, grated	

Add hot milk and margarine to sweet potatoes and beat until fluffy. Add lemon rind, salt, and pepper. Fold in stiffly beaten egg whites. Bake in greased casserole, 400 degrees, 35 minutes. 6 servings. *1 serving contains 21 grams carbohydrate.*

SCALLOPED POTATOES WITH CARROTS

3 cups potatoes, raw, sliced	2 teaspoons salt pepper, as desired
2 cups carrots, raw, thinly sliced	2 cups milk
1 large onion, raw, thinly sliced	1 tablespoon margarine or butter
2 tablespoons flour	paprika, sprinkling

Place alternating layers of potatoes, carrots, and onions in buttered casserole. Sprinkle each layer with some of the flour, salt, and pepper mixture. Add milk, dot with margarine or butter, and sprinkle with paprika. Bake until vegetables are tender, at 350 degrees for 2 hours. 6 servings. *1 serving contains 27 grams carbohydrate.*

SCALLOPED CARROTS

12 large carrots (3 cups) peeled, diced, and cooked until tender. Place in casserole and cover with the following sauce:

4 tablespoons butter
1 teaspoon salt
1 medium onion, diced
1½ teaspoons dry mustard
2 teaspoons celery flaked
2 cups milk
¼ cup flour
buttered bread crumbs
½ teaspoon pepper

Simmer onion and celery in butter. Add flour, pepper, salt, and dry mustard. Slowly add milk and stir until thick. Pour over carrots and cover with buttered bread crumbs. Bake at 350 degrees for one hour. Serves 6.

This is a super recipe for children who don't care for carrots. They'll love it—parents do too. *1 serving contains 19 grams carbohydrate.*

ASPARAGUS PAR EXCELLENCE

1 onion, peeled, chopped
2 teaspoons snipped
1 green pepper, seeded,
pimiento
chopped
½ teaspoon tarragon
2 teaspoons salt
2 teaspoons parsley
¼ teaspoon pepper
2 10-ounce packages
frozen asparagus
spears

In medium skillet, barely cover the chopped onion, green pepper, salt, and pepper with cold water. Over high heat bring to boil, then reduce heat to low and simmer 5 minutes. Lay frozen asparagus in skillet over low heat, cover. Simmer 10 to 15 minutes, or until tender. In serving dish arrange asparagus; surround with onion-pepper mixture; sprinkle with pimiento, tarragon, and parsley. Makes 6 servings. Carbohydrate does not need to be considered.

BROCCOLI SUPREME

1 egg, slightly beaten
1 10-ounce package frozen
   broccoli
1 8½-ounce can cream-
   style corn
1 tablespoon grated onion

¼ teaspoon salt
dash pepper
3 tablespoons margarine
   or butter
1 cup herb seasoned
   stuffing mix

Combine egg, broccoli, corn, onion, salt, and pepper. In saucepan melt butter or margarine; add herb seasoned stuffing mix, tossing to coat. Stir ¾ cup of the stuffing mix into vegetable mixture. Turn into ungreased 1-quart casserole. Sprinkle remaining stuffing mix on top. Bake, uncovered, in 350 degree oven for 35 to 40 minutes. 6 servings. *1 serving contains 14 grams carbohydrate.*

BROCCOLI PUFF

1 10-ounce package fro-
   zen broccoli cuts
1 can condensed Heinz
   Cream of Mushroom
   Soup
½ cup sharp process
   American cheese,
   shredded

¼ cup milk
¼ cup mayonnaise or salad
   dressing
1 egg, beaten
¼ cup fine dry bread
   crumbs
1 tablespoon butter,
   melted

Cook frozen broccoli according to package directions, omitting salt called for. Drain thoroughly. Place broccoli cuts in 10″ x 6″ x 1½″ baking dish. Stir together condensed soup and shredded cheese. Gradually add milk, mayonnaise, and beaten egg to soup mixture, stirring until well blended. Pour over broccoli in baking dish. Combine bread crumbs and melted butter; sprinkle evenly over soup mixture. Bake at 350 debrees for 45 minutes, until crumbs are lightly browned. Serves 6. *1 serving contains 7 grams carbohydrate.*

CORN SOUFFLÉ

5 tablespoons flour	½ cup milk, skim, scalded
½ teaspoon salt	6 eggs, separated
⅛ teaspoon pepper	1 cup corn, canned or
4 tablespoons shortening, melted	fresh

Blend flour and seasonings with melted shortening. Add milk gradually, stirring constantly. Add beaten egg yolks and corn. Finally, fold in stiffly beaten egg whites and pour into 2-quart casserole. Bake at 300 degrees for 1¼ hours. Serve immediately. 6 servings. *1 serving contains 14 grams carbohydrate.*

CORN PUDDING

2 cups drained whole kernel corn	2 eggs, well-beaten
1 teaspoon salt	1 cup skim milk
¼ teaspoon pepper	1 tablespoon butter
artificial sweetener equal to 1 teaspoon sugar, if desired	

Combine all ingredients and pour into casserole dish. Bake at 350 degrees for 60 to 70 minutes or until knife comes out clean when inserted in center of pudding. Divide pudding into 8 equal servings. *1 serving contains 15 grams carbohydrate.*

STUFFED CELERY

12 stalks celery, small	10 pimiento olives, chopped
¾ cup cottage cheese	
3 tablespoons cream, light	¼ teaspoon salt

Mix cheese, cream, olives, and salt thoroughly. Fill celery with mixture. Chill. 4 servings. *1 serving contains 5 grams carbohydrate.*

GREEN BEANS SORRENTO

1 strip bacon
¼ cup finely chopped onion
1 clove garlic, minced
2 tablespoons finely chopped green pepper
1 medium tomato, coarsely chopped
⅓ cup water
2 9-ounce packages frozen green beans partially thawed
½ teaspoon oregano
1¼ teaspoons salt
⅛ teaspoon pepper

Cut bacon into small pieces. In medium skillet (with tight fitting cover) over medium heat, sauté bacon until lightly browned. Add onion, garlic, and green pepper; sauté until golden. Stir in tomato pieces, green beans, oregano, salt, pepper, ⅓ cup water. Cover and simmer 5 to 10 minutes. Makes 6 servings. Carbohydrate does not need to be considered.

FRENCH GREEN BEANS, CELERY, AND ONIONS

3 slices bacon
1 cup celery, diced
1 tablespoon flour
½ cup milk, skim
¼ cup onion liquor
1 teaspoon salt
pepper
1 cup onions, boiled, chopped
2 cups green beans, French style, cooked

Fry bacon until crisp. Remove bacon and cook celery in hot fat until tender. Add flour and blend. Add milk and onion liquor, salt and pepper. Cook until thick, stirring constantly. Add drained onions and drained beans. Heat thoroughly. Pour into serving dish and garnish with broken bits of bacon. 6 servings. *1 serving contains 8 grams carbohydrate.*

GREEN BEANS WITH MUSHROOMS

2 cups green beans, cooked

2 tablespoons margarine, melted

½ teaspoon salt

1 cup mushrooms, sliced (or Heinz Mushroom Soup, one can)

⅓ cup cheese, grated

¼ cup cracker crumbs

Mix green beans, margarine, and salt. Place half the mixture in buttered casserole. Cover with mushrooms or mushroom soup. Add another layer of each. Top with grated cheese and cracker crumbs. If the mixture seems dry, add a little liquid from green beans or a small amount of milk. Heat until thoroughly warm at 350 degrees, about 30 minutes. 6 servings. *1 serving contains 6 grams carbohydrate. 1 serving with mushroom soup contains 10 grams carbohydrate.*

NOTE: Green beans mixed with 1 tablespoon prepared mustard and 1 tablespoon horseradish makes a tasty vegetable casserole.

CREOLE CABBAGE

3 cups green cabbage

½ pound sausage

1 large onion, chopped

1 clove garlic, minced

1 cup canned tomatoes

2 tablespoons green pepper, chopped

¼ teaspoon thyme

½ teaspoon salt

¼ teaspoon pepper

1 whole clove (optional)

1 bay leaf (optional)

Cook sausage in skillet. Add onion and garlic and brown. Pour off excess fat. Add tomatoes, green pepper, and seasonings and simmer 3 minutes. Add cabbage, cut into sixths. Cover and cook for 10 to 15 minutes. If clove and bay leaf are used, remove before serving. 6 servings. *1 serving contains 6 grams carbohydrate.*

CABBAGE WITH CARAWAY SEEDS

1 medium head cabbage (1½ to 2 pounds)	¼ cup water
	1 teaspoon butter, melted
1 teaspoon salt	½ teaspoon caraway seeds

Cut cabbage in six wedges. In large saucepan over medium heat, bring water and salt to a boil; add cabbage. Cook covered 7 to 11 minutes or until tender. Drain off remaining water; toss cabbage and remaining ingredients. Makes 6 servings. Carbohydrate does not need to be considered.

BAKED EGGPLANT

1 medium sized eggplant, pared, cut into ½" cubes	½ teaspoon garlic powder
	1 medium sized onion
1 pound can solid pack tomatoes	¼ pound fresh or canned mushrooms
1 small green pepper	½ teaspoon oregano
½ teaspoon salt	1 stalk celery

Parboil eggplant in small amount of water for 6 minutes. Drain. Combine other ingredients in a large bowl. Arrange tomato mixture and eggplant in layers beginning and ending with tomato mixture. Bake 1 hour at 350 degrees. Makes 4 servings. *1 serving contains 7 grams carbohydrate.*

BAKED EGGPLANT

2 cups cooked eggplant, medium size	2 tablespoons onion, minced
1 tablespoon margarine or butter	½ teaspoon salt
1 slice bread crumbs	⅛ teaspoon pepper
2 eggs, beaten	¼ cup pimiento, chopped
	few sprigs of parsley

Peel eggplant and cut crosswise in half-inch slices. Boil in salted water to cover until soft. Drain and mash. To eggplant, add margarine, bread crumbs, beaten eggs, onion, salt, pepper, and chopped pimiento. Pour mixture into greased casserole and bake at 400 degrees for 15 minutes. Serve garnished with sprigs of parsley. 4 servings. *1 serving contains 8 grams carbohydrate.*

SCALLOPED EGGPLANT

2 cups cooked eggplant, medium size	3 ounces cheese, grated
½ cup coarse cracker crumbs	1 egg, beaten
	½ cup milk, skim
4 tablespoons onion, minced	2 tablespoons margarine or butter

Peel eggplant and cut in 1-inch cubes. Cook in boiling salted water until tender (8 minutes). Drain. Put eggplant, half the cracker crumbs, onion, and cheese in layers in buttered casserole. Combine egg and milk and pour over other ingredients. Dot with margarine and sprinkle with remaining cracker crumbs. Bake at 350 degrees for 30 minutes. 6 servings. *1 serving contains 9 grams carbohydrate.*

PEAS ON TOAST

3 tablespoons margarine
   or butter
1 large onion, chopped
½ cup green pepper,
   chopped
½ cup mushrooms, sliced

2 cups peas, cooked
⅛ teaspoon pepper
¼ teaspoon salt
3 ounces cheese, grated
6 slices toast

Melt shortening in skillet and sauté onion, green pepper, and mushrooms. Heat peas in their own liquid. Drain off most of liquid and add to sautéed mixture with salt and pepper. Add grated cheese. When thoroughly heated, serve immediately on toast. 6 servings. *1 serving contains 22 grams carbohydrate.*

PEAS AND CELERY

⅓ cup coarsely chopped
   celery
1 10-ounce package
   frozen peas

½ cup water
½ teaspoon thyme leaves
¼ teaspoon salt

In covered medium saucepan over medium heat, cook celery in water for 5 minutes or until tender. Add peas, cover, and cook 8 to 10 minutes. Drain. Sprinkle peas with thyme and salt. Makes 4 servings. *½ cup serving contains 7 grams carbohydrate.*

MUSHROOMS Á LA SAUTERNE

1 pound fresh mushrooms,
   sliced
1 medium celery heart
1 bunch parsley
2 bunches green onions,
   all chopped fine (tops
   too)

1 cube butter
1 tablespoon Worcester-
   shire sauce
1 cup sauterne
salt and pepper to taste

Sauté seasoned vegetables in butter for 5 minutes. Add Worcestershire and sauterne. Mix well, cover, and simmer 15 minutes, stirring occasionally. Serve piping hot as meat garnish or vegetable dish. Serves 4 to 6 people. Carbohydrate does not need to be considered.

SPINACH PUDDING

2 10-ounce packages frozen
   chopped spinach
2 cups cottage cheese,
   drained in a sieve
1 teaspoon salt

⅓ cup Parmesan cheese,
   grated
2 eggs
additional Parmesan cheese

Cook spinach, following package directions, and drain thoroughly. Mix spinach, cottage cheese, salt, grated Parmesan cheese and eggs. Turn into buttered casserole. Bake at 350 degrees for 30 minutes. Serve with additional cheese. Serves 6. *1 serving contains 6 grams carbohydrate.*

CURRIED SPINACH

2 10-ounce packages fro-
   zen chopped spinach
1 teaspoon salt
⅛ teaspoon pepper

⅛ teaspoon nutmeg
¼ teaspoon curry powder
2 tablespoons butter

Cook spinach; add salt. Meanwhile in small saucepan, melt butter. Remove from heat, stir in pepper, nutmeg, and curry powder. Drain spinach well through fine strainer. Return to original pan, then quickly add butter mixture and toss. Makes 6 servings. Carbohydrate does not need to be considered.

SPINACH MOLD

1 large onion, sliced	2 cups milk, skim, scalded
4 tablespoons margarine	1 slice soft bread, crumbed
4 tablespoons flour	2 eggs, separated
1 teaspoon salt	3 cups spinach, cooked,
⅛ teaspoon pepper	chopped
paprika, as desired	

Brown onion in a little margarine. Make white sauce by blending together melted margarine, flour, and seasonings, adding scalded milk gradually, and cooking over hot water until thick. Add bread crumbs, slightly-beaten egg yolks, spinach, and onion. Fold in stiffly-beaten egg whites. Turn into greased mold and bake at 375 degrees for 30 minutes. Unmold on hot plate and serve immediately. 7 servings. *1 serving contains 13 grams carbohydrate.*

CREOLE SQUASH

5 slices bacon, chopped	½ cup tomatoes
1 large onion, chopped	½ teaspoon salt
3 cups summer squash,	⅛ teaspoon pepper
cubed	

Cook bacon a little and then add chopped onion and brown. Add squash, tomatoes, salt, and pepper. Cover and let simmer until tender (about 25 minutes). *1 serving contains 7 grams carbohydrate.*

WINTER SQUASH

3 cups winter squash,	3 eggs, beaten
cooked	1½ teaspoons salt
3 tablespoons margarine	pepper to taste
1 tablespoon onion, minced	few sprigs of parsley

Beat together squash, margarine, onion, eggs, salt, and pepper. Pour into greased ring mold and place in pan of water. Bake 350 degrees, 1 hour until firm. When ready to serve, turn onto hot serving dish and fill ring with peas, green beans, or other desired vegetable and garnish with parsley. 6 servings. *1 serving of squash contains 7 grams carbohydrate.*

FLUFFY ACORN SQUASH

2 acorn squash, cut in
   halves
1 tablespoon skimmed or
   reliquified non-fat dry
   milk

½ teaspoon cinnamon
¼ to ½ teaspoon allspice
½ teaspoon salt

Preheat oven to 400 degrees. On large cookie sheet, place squash cut side down; bake 30 minutes or until tender. Remove from oven and cool slightly. With spoon, carefully scoop squash from shells into medium bowl. Reserve 2 shells. Mash squash. Beat in remaining ingredients. Refill reserved shells. If desired sprinkle lightly with cinnamon. *½ cup serving contains 7 grams carbohydrate.*

BAKED SQUASH

squash (acorn or Hubbard)
salt and pepper

1 teaspoon butter

Wash squash. Without cutting, bake for about 30 minutes at 400 degrees. Cut squash in serving size pieces, remove seeds, and season with salt, pepper, butter. Put pieces on a shallow pan, and continue baking for 20 to 30 minutes until very tender.

A medium acorn squash will serve 2 persons, while a Hubbard squash depending upon size, will provide 6 or more servings. *½ cup contains 7 grams carbohydrate.*

HARVARD BEETS

1 cup cooked or canned beets	½ tablespoon cornstarch
	¼ teaspoon salt
2½ Sucaryl tablets	2 tablespoons cider vinegar
2 tablespoons water	

Dice or slice beets. Mash Sucaryl tablets and dissolve in water. Combine cornstarch, salt, vinegar, and dissolved Sucaryl tablets. Cook over low heat until thickened, stirring constantly. Add beets. Heat until beets are hot. Serve at once. 2 servings. *1 serving contains 7 grams carbohydrate.*

PICKLED BEETS

2½ cups cooked or canned beets, sliced	1 bay leaf
	4 saccharin tablets (¼ grain each) or
⅓ cup vinegar	
½ teaspoon salt	3 to 4 Sucaryl tablets (⅛ gram each)
4 whole cloves	

Drain liquid from beets into saucepan. Add remaining ingredients and bring to boil. Pour over beets. Chill about 6 hours before serving. Can be served cold or reheated. 5 servings. *½ cup contains 3 grams carbohydrate.*

ORANGE GLAZED BEETS

2 tablespoons butter or margarine	1 teaspoon cider vinegar
	2 teaspoons grated orange rind
2 teaspoons cornstarch	
¼ teaspoon salt	½ cup orange juice
1 tablespoon Sucaryl solution	3 cups cooked sliced beets (1½ pounds)

Melt butter in saucepan. Blend in cornstarch and salt. Add Sucaryl, vinegar, orange rind and juice. Cook over medium heat until smooth and thick, stirring constantly.

Add beets and simmer over low heat about 10 minutes until heated through. 6 servings. *1 serving contains 7 grams carbohydrate.*

WHOLE TOMATO STUFFED WITH RICE

1 medium size tomato	1 teaspoon butter
2 tablespoons rice	salt and pepper

Remove the center from the tomato, dust the inside with salt and very little pepper, and set aside. Boil the rice for about 20 minutes, drain, and add the tomato pulp, butter, salt, and pepper. Fill the center with rice. Set the tomato in a lightly buttered pan, and bake in a moderate oven 20 minutes. Carbohydrate does not need to be considered.

BROILED TOMATO

1 teaspoon butter	salt and pepper
1 tablespoon fine bread crumbs	1 tomato

Melt butter, brown bread crumbs, and season with salt and pepper. Wash tomato, remove core end, and cut in half. Dust with salt and pepper, and sprinkle bread crumbs on each half. Place on greased broiler rack about 3 inches below direct flame. Broil for about 10 minutes or until tender. Carbohydrate does not need to be considered.

SAVORY STEWED TOMATOES

1 can (1 lb., 4 oz.) or 2¼ cups fresh cooked tomatoes	2 tablespoons grated onion
	4 whole cloves
1 tablespoon minced green pepper	½ teaspoon curry powder
	salt and pepper

Combine all ingredients. Simmer 5 minutes. 5 servings. Carbohydrate does not need to be considered.

BAKED CHEESE TOMATOES

6 large, firm tomatoes
½ lb. (or less) mild Cheddar cheese, cubed
1 cup toasted bread cubes (2 slices)
1 teaspoon basil
½ teaspoon salt
1 tablespoon parsley flakes
½ cup chopped cashew nuts
2 tablespoons butter, melted
½ cup finely chopped onion
1 cup diced tomato pulp

Core tomatoes and scoop out pulp, leaving a sturdy shell. Sprinkle lightly with salt. Combine cheese, bread cubes, basil, salt, parsley, nuts, butter, onion, and tomato pulp. Fill tomatoe shells with cheese mixture. Bake at 350 degrees, covered, for about 30 minutes, or until cheese melts. Serves 6.

Variation: Tomatoes may also be cooked on a grill 15 to 30 minutes, depending on fire. *1 serving contains 9 grams carbohydrate.*

OKRA AND TOMATOES

1 can (1 pound) cut okra
1 can (8 ounces) stewed tomatoes
½ teaspoon dried crushed basil

Heat okra in its liquid, drain, and return to saucepan. Add tomatoes and basil and reheat. Makes 4 servings. Carbohydrate does not need to be considered.

BAKED TOMATOES SUPREME

2 large ripe tomatoes
4 drops liquid sweetener
1 tablespoon minced scallion
1 tablespoon minced parsley

Slice tomatoes in half. Place half on large square of double thick foil. Sprinkle with sweetener, minced scallions, and parsley. Bring foil up and around tomato half. Seal edge of foil but leave space at top for steaming. Bake at 350 degrees for 20 minutes. Makes 4 servings. Carbohydrate does not need to be considered.

BAKED ZUCCHINI AND PEAS

1 10½-ounce can mushroom soup
½ pound mushrooms, sliced
2 tablespoons butter
5 zucchini, sliced

1 10½-ounce package peas, partially defrosted
1 jar (4 oz.) salted pumpkin seeds

Cook mushrooms in butter until lightly browned. Arrange a layer of mushrooms in buttered casserole, then a layer of zucchini. Spread with some of the mushroom soup. Add a layer of peas. Repeat until all vegetables are used, reserving a little of the soup for the top. Spread remaining soup over casserole. Cover and bake at 350 degrees for 30 minutes. Remove casserole from oven and cover thickly with pumpkin seeds. Bake uncovered 15 minutes longer. Serves 8. *1 serving contains 7 grams carbohydrate.*

STUFFED GREEN PEPPERS

6 medium green peppers
1 pound lean ground beef
⅓ cup onion, chopped
½ teaspoon salt
dash pepper
1-pound can tomatoes
½ cup water
½ cup uncooked long-grain rice

1½ tablespoons chopped parsley
1 teaspoon Worcestershire sauce
sugar substitute to taste, if desired

Cut off tops of 6 medium green peppers; remove seeds and membrane. Precook green pepper shells in boiling salted water about 5 minutes. Drain. Sprinkle inside of shells generously with salt. Cook ground beef and onion until meat is lightly browned. Season with ¼ teaspoon salt and dash pepper. Add tomatoes, water, rice, and Worcestershire sauce. Cover and simmer until rice is tender, about 15 minutes. Stuff peppers; stand upright in 10″ x 6″ x 1½″ baking dish. Bake uncovered at 350 degrees for 20 to 25 minutes. Makes 6 servings. *1 serving contains 15 grams carbohydrate.*

STUFFED PEPPERS

2 tablespoons cooking oil	1 teaspoon salt
12 ounces ground beef, veal or chicken	¼ teaspoon pepper
	4 slices soft bread, crumbed
1 large onion, chopped	
2 cups tomatoes, canned	3 green peppers

Brown beef and onions in cooking oil. Add tomatoes, salt, and pepper. Simmer 30 minutes. Cut peppers in half, remove seeds, and cook in boiling water 3 minutes. Drain. Add bread crumbs and fill pepper halves with mixture. Arrange on greased baking pan. Bake 350 degrees, 30 minutes. 6 servings. *1 serving contains 15 grams carbohydrate.*

NOTE: Ground ham may be substituted for some of the beef. Mushrooms may be added or substituted for tomatoes.

Desserts

FRESH FRUIT CUP

Any fruits may be combined to make a fruit cup. One half cup of mixed fruits equals *1 serving. 10 grams carbohydrate.*

Examples: orange, grapefruit, pineapple; apple, grapefruit, strawberries; peach, orange, blackberries; grapes, orange, melon; melon, grapefruit, banana.

FLAMING CHERRIES JUBILEE

1 can (16 ounce) sugar free dark cherries
2 teaspoons cornstarch
1 teaspoon sugar
½ teaspoon artificial liquid sweetener
¼ cup cherry brandy
red food coloring
¼ cup cherry kirsch (to flame)

Drain cherries. Add water to cherry liquid to make ¾ cup. In a saucepan, combine cornstarch and sugar; blend in cherry liquid. Cook and stir until thickened. Add cherries, liquid sweetener, cherry brandy, and few drops of food color.

To flame, slowly heat cherry kirsch in small saucepan for a few minutes. *Do not boil.* Light with match and pour over cherries (be sure cherry mixture is hot). Serves 6. *1 serving contains 10 grams carbohydrate.*

GINGER PEAR HALVES

½ cup liquid drained from pears (dietetic packed)
1 saccharin tablet (¼ grain) or 1 Sucaryl tablet (⅛ grain)
¼ teaspoon ginger
2 pear halves, drained

Combine all ingredients except pear halves. Heat to boiling. Add pear halves. Cover and let stand in hot liquid for at least a half hour. Serve hot or chilled. *1 serving contains 10 grams carbohydrate.*

CHEESE APPLE CRISP

4 medium apples, cored and sliced
¼ cup water
½ teaspoon lemon juice
4½ teaspoons liquid Sucaryl
½ cup flour
½ teaspoon salt
½ teaspoon cinnamon
3 tablespoons butter or margarine
½ cup grated Cheddar cheese

Preheat oven to 350 degrees. Place sliced apples in a deep pie plate or a shallow baking dish. Combine water, lemon juice, and Sucaryl. Pour over apples. Combine flour, salt, and cinnamon; cut in margarine until of consistency of coarse corn meal; sprinkle over apples. Cover with grated cheese. Bake 30 to 40 minutes. *1 serving contains 21 grams carbohydrate. If the apples are small, 1 serving contains 11 grams carbohydrate.*

BAKED APPLE

Core and peel ½ inch of skin from top of 1 apple. Turn top side down in small baking dish. Pour half cup cherry flavor low calorie soda over. Bake in 350 degree oven for 45 minutes. *1 serving contains 10 grams carbohydrate.*

APPLE BETTY

4 medium sized apples, pared, cored, sliced
¼ teaspoon cinnamon
½ cup graham cracker crumbs
1 tablespoon margarine, melted
¾ cup hot water
2 packages granulated sugar substitute
1 teaspoon lemon juice

Place apples in a 6-cup shallow baking dish. Mix in artificial sweetener and cinnamon. Toss to mix. Toss graham cracker crumbs with melted margarine in small bowl. Pour in hot water and add to apples; cover. Bake in a 400 degree oven for 15 minutes. Uncover and bake 15 minutes longer or until apples are tender. Serve warm. 6 servings. *1 serving contains 25 grams carbohydrate.*

RHUBARB WITH APPLES

1 pound rhubarb
4 small apples
2 teaspoons lemon rind, grated
½ teaspoon Sucaryl solution
sprinkling of cinnamon

Cut rhubarb into one-inch pieces. Peel and slice apples. Mix rhubarb, apples, lemon rind, and Sucaryl solution in casserole. Sprinkle with cinnamon. Cover tightly and bake until soft at 350 degrees about 40 minutes. 6 servings. *1 serving contains 10 grams carbohydrate.*

PEACH COBBLER

2 cups peaches, fresh
1 teaspoon lemon rind, grated
1 tablespoon lemon juice
½ teaspoon almond extract
1 cup flour
1½ teaspoons baking powder
½ teaspoon salt
2 tablespoons margarine
⅜ cup milk
½ teaspoon Sucaryl solution

Arrange peaches in 8″ square baking dish. Sprinkle with mixture of lemon rind, lemon juice, and almond extract. Sift together flour, baking powder, and salt. Cut in margarine until mixture is like coarse crumbs. Stir in milk and Sucaryl solution, just until flour is moistened. Roll out dough into 8″ square. Spread crust over peaches. Bake at 450 degrees for 30 minutes. 6 servings. *1 serving contains 25 grams carbohydrate.*

BREAD PUDDING

1 cup dry bread cubes (3 slices)
1½ cups skim milk, scalded
2 tablespoons raisins
2 teaspoons liquid sweetener
½ teaspoon cinnamon
2 eggs, lightly beaten
1 teaspoon vanilla extract

Soak bread cubes in scalded milk for 5 minutes. Add liquid sweetener, cinnamon, and raisins. Pour bread mixture slowly over beaten eggs; add vanilla and blend well. Pour into greased baking dish. Bake in 325 degree oven for 50 minutes until firm. 4 servings. *1 serving contains 21 grams carbohydrate.*

BAKED CUSTARD

2 cups milk	1 teaspoon vanilla
2 eggs	extract
¼ teaspoon salt	sprinkling nutmeg
1½ teaspoons Sucaryl solution	

Scald milk. Beat eggs slightly. Add salt and pour on slowly the scalded milk. Add Sucaryl solution and vanilla. Strain and pour into custard cups. Sprinkle with nutmeg. Set the cups in a pan of hot water and bake in 325 degree oven for 45 minutes or until a knife inserted in the custard comes out clean. 4 servings. *1 serving contains 6 grams carbohydrate.*

PUMPKIN CUSTARD

1 envelope gelatin	½ teaspoon cinnamon
¼ cup water	½ teaspoon nutmeg
3 eggs, separated	½ teaspoon salt
1¼ cups pumpkin, canned	1 tablespoon Sucaryl
½ cup milk, skim	solution
½ teaspoon ginger	

Sprinkle gelatin on cold water and let stand 5 minutes. Put egg yolks into the top of a double boiler and beat slightly. Add pumpkin, milk, spice, salt and Sucaryl solution and cook until thick. Add soaked gelatin and cool thoroughly. Fold in egg whites which have been beaten stiff. Pour into molds and cool in the refrigerator. 6 servings. *1 serving contains 4 grams carbohydrate.*

FLOATING ISLAND

½ cup milk	artificial sweetener, if
1 egg	desired
¼ teaspoon vanilla extract	

Heat the milk in upper part of double boiler over boiling water. Beat the egg yolk in bowl, using rotary beater. Pour the hot milk over the yolk, mix well, and pour back into top part of the double boiler. Stir mixture constantly until it begins to thicken, about 10 minutes. Remove from heat; add vanilla and artificial sweetener, if used. Beat egg white stiff. When ready to serve the custard, place in glass dish and top with beaten egg white. If desired, it may be placed under the broiler for a few seconds to brown. *1 serving contains 6 grams carbohydrate.*

FRUIT CREAM

1 egg, beaten
½ cup water
3 ounces frozen orange or other fruit juice concentrate, partially defrosted
Sucaryl solution to taste

½ cup milk, powder, skim

Combine ingredients in order given, beating constantly until thick. Pour into freezing tray and freeze until firm. 5 servings. *1 serving contains 11 grams carbohydrate.*

TAPIOCA CREAM

1 egg, separated
2 cups milk
3 tablespoons tapioca
⅛ teaspoon salt

½ teaspoon vanilla extract
1 teaspoon Sucaryl solution

Mix egg yolk with a small amount of milk in a saucepan. Add remaining milk, tapioca, and salt. Cook over medium heat until mixture comes to a boil, stirring constantly (5 to 8 minutes). Beat egg white until it stands in soft peaks and then add to hot tapioca mixture. Add vanilla and Sucaryl solution. Cool. Stir again in 20 minutes. 4 servings. *1 serving contains 13 grams carbohydrate.*

CHOCOLATE SPANISH CREAM

1 envelope gelatin	¼ teaspoon salt
¼ cup water	1½ teaspoons Sucaryl
4 tablespoons cocoa	solution
2 eggs, separated	1 teaspoon vanilla
2 cups milk	extract

Soften gelatin in cold water for 5 minutes. Put cocoa in a double boiler, add a little milk to make a smooth paste, then add remaining milk and scald. Pour scalded milk mixture on slightly beaten egg yolks, stirring constantly. Add gelatin, salt, and Sucaryl solution and return to double boiler. Cook until mixture coats spoon. Add vanilla. Pour into bowl and chill until slightly thickened. Fold in stiffly-beaten egg whites. Pour into molds or sherbet glasses. Chill until firm. 6 servings. *1 serving contains 6 grams carbohydrate.*

ORANGE TAPIOCA

2 cups buttermilk	½ teaspoon Sucaryl
½ teaspoon baking soda	solution
3 tablespoons Minute	1 egg, separated
tapioca	¼ cup orange juice
	rind from 1 orange

Heat buttermilk and soda in double boiler. Add tapioca and Sucaryl solution and cook 15 minutes. Add beaten egg yolk and cook 5 minutes, stirring constantly. Cool. Add orange juice and rind. Fold in stiffly-beaten egg white. Pour into sherbet glasses and garnish each with orange section or slice. Chill. 4 servings. *1 serving contains 14 grams carbohydrate.*

PINEAPPLE AND RICE

¾ cup evaporated milk
1 envelope gelatin
1 cup boiled rice
½ cup pineapple, crushed,
  unsweetened

1 teaspoon Sucaryl
  solution
dash salt
¼ cup whipping cream

Chill ½ cup evaporated milk. Soften gelatin in remaining ¼ cup evaporated milk and dissolve over hot water. Add dissolved gelatin to rice. Add pineapple, Sucaryl solution, and salt. Whip chilled evaporated milk until stiff and fold into rice mixture. Pour into refrigerator tray and freeze until firm. Serve with a topping of whipped cream. 4 servings. *1 serving contains 19 grams carbohydrate.*

RICE PUDDING

2 eggs
1½ teaspoons Sucaryl
¼ teaspoon salt

1 teaspoon vanilla
2½ cups boiled rice
2 cups milk

Beat eggs slightly and add Sucaryl solution, salt, and vanilla. Add rice and milk. Pour into greased baking dish and place it in a shallow pan of water. Bake at 350 degrees for 1 hour. 8 servings. *1 serving contains 17 grams carbohydrate.*

COTTAGE PUDDING

2 eggs
¼ cup sugar
2 teaspoons Sucaryl
  solution
1 teaspoon vanilla extract

1 cup flour
1 teaspoon baking powder
¼ teaspoon salt
1 tablespoon margarine
½ cup milk

Beat eggs until thick. While continuing to beat, add sugar, Sucaryl solution, and vanilla. Mix and sift together flour, baking powder, and salt and add to egg mixture. Bring milk and margarine to boiling point and add mixture all at once. Pour into greased layer cake tin and bake in 350 degree oven for 35 minutes. Serve hot or cold with lemon sauce. 8 servings. *1 serving contains 17 grams carbohydrate.*

CHOCOLATE BREAD PUDDING

2 eggs	2 squares chocolate,
3 cups milk, skim	unsweetened, grated
2½ slices bread, crumbed	1 teaspoon vanilla extract
¼ teaspoon salt	1 tablespoon Sucaryl
	solution

In top of double boiler, beat eggs and add milk, bread crumbs, salt and grated chocolate. Cook over hot water until thick. Add vanilla and Sucaryl solution. Cool. Whipped cream may be used as a topping. 8 servings. *1 serving contains 11 grams carbohydrate.*

COCONUT BREAD PUDDING

2 cups milk, skim	¼ teaspoon salt
2 slices bread, crumbed	¼ cup coconut
2 eggs, slightly beaten	½ teaspoon vanilla extract
1 teaspoon Sucaryl solution	

Scald milk. Add bread crumbs. Beat eggs slightly. Add Sucaryl solution and salt. Add milk and bread slowly to egg mixture. Add coconut and vanilla. Pour into a buttered casserole. Place in pan of warm water and bake at 350 degrees for 1¼ hours. 4 servings. *1 serving contains 16 grams carbohydrate.*

SNOW PUDDING

1 envelope gelatin	1 cup hot water
¼ cup water	¼ cup lemon juice
½ tablespoon Sucaryl solution	1 teaspoon lemon rind
¼ teaspoon salt	2 egg whites

Soften gelatin in cold water. Add Sucaryl solution, salt, and hot water and stir until dissolved. Add lemon juice and rind. Cool. When nearly set, beat until frothy. Fold in stiffly beaten egg whites. Pour into molds. Unmold when time to serve. 6 servings. *1 serving contains 5 grams carbohydrate.*

PRUNE PUDDING

16 medium prunes	½ teaspoon cinnamon
2 cups milk, skim	¼ teaspoon nutmeg
3 tablespoons margarine	¼ teaspoon allspice
2 slices bread, crumbed	1 teaspoon salt
1 teaspoon Sucaryl solution	1 teaspoon vanilla extract
	2 eggs, slightly beaten

Cover prunes with boiling water and cook until tender. Drain, saving juice. Remove pits and chop very fine. Add one-fourth cup prune juice to chopped fruit. Scald milk. Add margarine, crumbs, Sucaryl solution, spices, salt, vanilla, eggs, and prunes. Turn into buttered 9″ square casserole. Set in pan of hot water and bake, 325 degrees for 45 minutes. Serve hot or cold. Garnish with whipped cream if desired. 6 servings. *1 serving contains 33 grams carbohydrate.*

VANILLA RUM PUDDING

Prepare 1 envelope (4 serving size) low calorie vanilla pudding and pie filling with 2 cups non-fat or whole milk as directed on package. Stir in ½ teaspoon rum extract before cooling. Makes about 2 cups or 4 servings. *½ cup serving contains 9 grams carbohydrate.*

SNOW-CAPPED RAINBOW DESSERT

1 envelope each lemon, lime, and cherry low calorie gelatin

1 envelope low calorie whipped topping

Prepare each envelope of gelatin in 1¾ cups water. Refrigerate in separate rectangular dishes. Then cut into ½" cubes. Pile equal portions of each color into 6 dessert dishes. Add ⅓ cup whipped topping. Then arrange a little triangle made with 3 cubes, all different colors, on top of the snowy pudding. 6 servings. Carbohydrate does not need to be considered.

LEMON SNOW

1 envelope unflavored gelatin
½ cup cold water
2 teaspoons grated lemon rind

¼ cup lemon juice
1¼ cups very hot water
artificial sweetener (equal to 1 teaspoon sugar)
1 egg white

Sprinkle gelatin on the cold water to soften. Add lemon rind and lemon juice to the very hot water. Bring to a boil. Remove from heat; add softened gelatin and sweetener and stir until completely dissolved. Chill to unbeaten egg white consistency. Add unbeaten egg white; beat with a rotary beater until fluffy. Place container in bowl of ice or ice water. Beat until mixture begins to hold its shape. Turn into one large mold (3 to 4 cup) or 6 individual molds. Chill until firm.

CHERRY FRAPPE

1 envelope low calorie cherry flavor gelatin
½ cup boiling water
5 maraschino cherries

2½ cups crushed ice
1 tablespoon maraschino cherry syrup

Place gelatin and boiling water in blender. Blend until gelatin is dissolved. Add cherries and syrup and continue to blend until mixture is fluffy. Add crushed ice and blend until mixture is the consistency of ice cream, about 3 to 4 minutes. Serve at once in a cup or glass. Or pour into 6 ounce paper cups and freeze for future use. Remove frozen frappes from freezer 15 minutes before serving. Garnish with mint, if desired. *1 serving contains 15 grams carbohydrate.*

SPRING PARFAIT

1¼ ounce envelope low calorie pudding mix	2 cups skim milk
	2 pints strawberries

Prepare pudding as directed on label. Cover surface with waxed paper. This may be done ahead of time. Before serving: with spoon, beat pudding until light and fluffy. Reserve 4 strawberries for garnish. Slice remaining berries crosswise. In 4 parfait glasses alternate layers of pudding and strawberries. Garnish with berries. 4 servings. *1 serving contains 22 grams carbohydrate.*

PEACH CHARLOTTE

1 envelope gelatin	½ teaspoon Sucaryl solution
¼ cup water	
1 8-ounce can peaches, water packed	6 crackers, graham, crushed
½ cup skim milk powder	½ cup coffee cream or ¼ cup whipping cream
¼ cup water	

Soak gelatin in water. Drain peaches. Add enough water to peach juice to make one-half cup liquid. Bring to boil. Add gelatin and stir until dissolved. Let stand until syrupy. Mash peaches to puree consistency and add to gelatin mixture. Beat milk powder and water to whipped cream consistency, add Sucaryl solution, and fold into gelatin mixture. Spread half cracker crumbs over bottoms of individual dessert dishes, cover with gelatin mixture and top with remainder of crumbs. Chill until serving time. Top with cream. 4 servings. *1 serving contains 23 grams carbohydrate.*

LEMON GELATIN

1 teaspoon unflavored   1 tablespoon lemon juice
      gelatin   ½ cup water
2 tablespoons cold water

Put cold water in top of double boiler add gelatin. Let stand 10 minutes at room temperature. Place pan over boiling water to dissolve gelatin. If desired as sweetener equal to 1 teaspoon sugar. Remove from stove. Add lemon juice and ½ cup water. Chill. You may use coffee (½ cup) in place of the water and then omit the lemon juice. Carbohydrate does not need to be considered.

STRAWBERRY BAVARIAN

1 envelope unflavored   artificial sweetener equal to
      gelatin   2 teaspoons sugar
½ cup cold water   ½ cup mashed, ripe straw-
½ teaspoon lemon rind   berries
1 cup very hot water   ⅓ cup undiluted evapo-
2 teaspoons lemon juice   rated milk

Sprinkle gelatin on the cold water to soften. Add lemon rind to the very hot water and boil for 2 minutes. Add softened gelatin to the lemon water and stir until thoroughly dissolved. Add lemon juice and sweetener. Strain and chill to unbeaten egg white consistency. Fold in mashed strawberries and whipped evaporated milk. Pile in individual serving dishes or turn into one large mold (3 to 4 cup). Chill until firm. Evaporated milk *must* be ice cold before whipping. *⅔ cup serving contains 5 grams carbohydrate.*

FRUIT COCKTAIL WHIP

1 teaspoon unflavored
    gelatin
2 tablespoons cold water
½ cup boiling water
artificial sweetener equal to
    2 teaspoons sugar

½ cup fruit cocktail, die-
    tetic canned or water
    packed
1 tablespoon lemon juice

  Sprinkle gelatin over cold water, let stand 5 minutes. Add boiling water, stir until dissolved. Add lemon juice and sweetener. Chill until mixture begins to set. Beat with rotary beater until fluffy; fold in fruit cocktail. Chill until firm. *1 serving contains 10 grams carbohydrate.* For a jellied fruit salad omit the beating.

COFFEE-ALMOND WHIP

1 teaspoon unflavored
    gelatin
2 tablespoons cold water
artificial sweetener to equal
    3 teaspoons sugar

½ cup hot coffee
⅛ teaspoon nutmeg
¼ teaspoon almond extract

  Sprinkle gelatin over cold water; let stand 5 minutes. Add boiling coffee; stir until dissolved. Add remaining ingredients. Chill until mixture begins to set. Beat until fluffy with rotary beater. Chill until firm. Carbohydrate does not need to be considered.

PRUNE WHIP

1 envelope gelatin
¼ cup water
artificial sweetener to equal
    ¼ cup sugar
¼ teaspoon salt
¾ cup hot prune juice

12 prunes, pulped or
    mashed
2 tablespoons lemon juice
2 egg whites
12 pecan meats, chopped

Sprinkle gelatin on cold water and let stand five minutes. Add to mixture of sweetener, salt, and hot prune juice. Stir until dissolved. Add prune pulp and lemon juice. Cool. When mixture begins to thicken, fold in stiffly beaten egg whites. Pile gently by spoonfuls into sherbet glasses and sprinkle with nuts. 6 servings. *1 serving contains 18 grams carbohydrate.*

MOCHA FLUFF

1 envelope gelatin	¼ teaspoon salt
¼ cup water	1⅓ cups hot, strong coffee
1½ teaspoons Sucaryl Solution or artificial sweetener to equal ¼ cup sugar	2 tablespoons lemon juice
	2 egg whites, stiffly beaten

Soften gelatin in cold water. Add sweetener, salt and hot coffee, stirring thoroughly to dissolve. Add lemon juice. Cool. When nearly set, beat until stiff. Add egg whites and continue beating until mixture holds its shape. Turn into molds and chill. 4 servings. Carbohydrate does not need to be considered.

TOMATO JUICE SHERBET

2 tablespoons unflavored gelatin	3 tablespoons fresh lemon juice
¼ cup water	¾ teaspoon salt
7 cups fresh or canned tomato juice	¼ teaspoon white pepper
	3 egg whites

Soften gelatin in water. In saucepan heat tomato juice to a boil. Remove from heat. Add softened gelatin, lemon juice, salt, and pepper to the hot juice. Cool. Beat the egg whites until stiff and then stir into the tomato mixture. Churn-freeze. Half-gallon. Carbohydrate does not need to be considered.

TOMATO SHERBET

1 quart can tomatoes, drained or 12 fresh tomatoes
1 slice of onion
¼ teaspoon ground mace
1 teaspoon celery seed
2 cups water
1 teaspoon salt
1 teaspoon paprika
1 tablespoon unflavored gelatin
1 tablespoon fresh lemon juice
⅛ teaspoon cayenne pepper

In saucepan, combine all ingredients. Bring to a boil and boil for 5 minutes. Stirring occasionally, strain and cool. Churn-freeze. Half-gallon. Carbohydrate does not need to be considered.

CHOCOLATE ICE CREAM

¾ cup milk, powder, skim
3 tablespoons cocoa
½ cup water
1 teaspoon Sucaryl solution
½ teaspoon vanilla

Mix milk powder and cocoa thoroughly. Sprinkle on top of mixture of Sucaryl solution, water, and vanilla. Beat until smooth and pour into refrigerator tray. Freeze until firm. 4 servings. *1 serving contains 12 grams carbohydrate.*

FRUIT ICE

½ cup orange juice or ⅓ cup pineapple juice
1 tablespoon lemon juice
1 egg white
½ cup water

Combine fruit juices and water and freeze. Stir mixture often while freezing. When almost hard, fold in 1 stiffly beaten egg white. Place in individual mold. Allow to set. *1 serving contains 10 grams carbohydrate.*

PINEAPPLE SHERBET

1 envelope gelatin
⅓ cup pineapple juice
1 cup pineapple, crushed, without juice
2 cups buttermilk

artificial sweetener equal to ½ cup sugar
1 teaspoon vanilla extract
1 egg white

Soften gelatin in pineapple juice and dissolve over hot water. Combine crushed pineapple, buttermilk, sweetener, vanilla, and gelatin. Fold in stiffly beaten egg white. Pour into refrigerator tray and freeze until firm. Stir twice while freezing. 6 servings. *1 serving contains 11 grams carbohydrate.*

ICE CREAM PARLEE

¼ cup ice cream, any flavor
¼ of a small banana, sliced

1 tablespoon pecan meats, chopped

Top the ice cream with banana and nuts. *1 serving contains 7 grams carbohydrate.*

ORANGE ICE

1 cup orange juice, fresh or made from frozen concentrate
1 teaspoon unflavored gelatin
2 tablespoons lemon juice

1 tablespoon grated orange peel
artificial sweetener equal to ½ cup sugar
½ cup dry milk powder, skim

At least 3½ hours before serving: In small saucepan, pour ¼ cup orange juice. Sprinkle in gelatin and cook over low heat, stirring constantly until gelatin is dissolved. Remove from heat; stir in remaining orange juice, lemon juice, orange peel, and sweetener. Cool. In small bowl with mixer at high speed, beat milk powder with ½ cup ice water until stiff peaks form, with rubber spatula, gently stir in gelatin mixture until well-combined. Pour into shallow pan; freeze 3 hours or until firm. 8 servings. *1 serving contains 7 grams carbohydrate.*

Cakes, Pies, Cookies

APPLESAUCE CUPCAKES

½ cup shortening
1 egg
2 teaspoons liquid
   sweetener
1¾ cups sifted cake flour
1 teaspoon baking soda
¼ teaspoon salt
1 teaspoon cinnamon

¼ teaspoon each: cloves,
   allspice, ginger
1 cup unsweetened apple-
   sauce
½ teaspoon lemon juice
1 teaspoon vanilla
⅓ cup raisins

Preheat oven to 375 degrees. Cream shortening until
fluffy. Beat egg and sugar substitute until lemon colored;
add to shortening and blend well. Sift together all dry ingredients, add to shortening mixture alternately with applesauce, blending well after each addition. Add vanilla
and lemon juice; stir in raisins. Line 2 small cupcake pans

with paper baking cups; pour batter in ⅔ full and bake 15 to 20 minutes. If paper cups are not used, grease the cupcake pans very lightly. Makes 12 servings. *1 cupcake contains 15 grams carbohydrate.*

ORANGE SPONGE CAKE

7 eggs, separated
½ cup orange juice
1 tablespoon grated orange rind
3 tablespoons liquid Sucaryl

2 tablespoons lemon juice
½ teaspoon vanilla
1½ cups sifted cake flour
¼ teaspoon salt
¾ teaspoon cream of tartar

Preheat oven to 325 degrees. Have eggs at room temperature for best volume when beaten. On high speed of mixer, beat egg yolks until thick and lemon-colored, 5 minutes. Combine orange juice, orange rind, Sucaryl, lemon juice, and vanilla. Combine sifted cake flour and salt; beat into yolks alternately with liquid. Beat egg whites until foamy; add cream of tartar and beat until stiff peaks form. Fold batter gently into the stiffly beaten egg whites. Pour into an ungreased 9″ tube pan. Bake 65 minutes, or until done. Invert cake to cool. 12 servings. *1 serving contains 11 grams carbohydrate.*

GOLDEN CAKE

1 cup flour, sifted
1½ teaspoons baking powder
½ teaspoon salt
¼ cup cooking oil
3 egg yolks

½ cup frozen orange juice concentrate (un-sweetened)
1 tablespoon Sucaryl solution
4 egg whites
¼ teaspoon cream of tartar

Mix and sift dry ingredients thoroughly (several times). Make a well in mixture. Add, in order, cooking oil, unbeaten egg yolks, orange concentrate, and Sucaryl solution. Beat until smooth. Place egg whites in large bowl, add cream of tartar, and beat until stiff. Pour egg yolk mixture gradually over egg whites and gently fold in. Pour into 9" tube pan and bake at 325 degrees for 35 minutes. 10 servings. *1 serving contains 12 grams carbohydrate.*

CHOCOLATE ICE BOX CAKE

½ cup cocoa
½ teaspoon salt
1½ cups evaporated milk

1½ teaspoons Sucaryl solution
½ teaspoon vanilla
16 graham crackers

Blend together cocoa, salt, evaporated milk, and Sucaryl solution in top of double boiler. Cook over hot water until thick, stirring frequently. Add vanilla and cool. Line refrigerator tray with waxed paper. Place 4 graham crackers on bottom of tray. Cover with 3 layers each of chocolate mixture and graham crackers, respectively. Chill in freezing unit of refrigerator until firm. 6 servings. *1 serving contains 30 grams carbohydrate.*

CHERRY UP-SIDE-DOWN CAKE

2 cups red tart cherries (or other fruit)
2 tablespoons margarine
¼ cup sugar
1 egg
1¼ cups flour, sifted

2 teaspoons baking powder
¼ teaspoon salt
½ cup milk
¼ teaspoon almond extract
1 teaspoon Sucaryl solution

Drain cherries and save juice for making cherry sauce. Spread cherries over bottom of greased shallow loaf pan. Cream margarine with sugar. Add egg and beat well. Mix and sift flour, baking powder, and salt, and add alternately with milk to first mixture. Add flavoring and Su-caryl solution. Pour batter over cherries and bake at 350 degrees for 50 minutes. Serve warm with cherry sauce. 8 servings. *1 serving contains 26 grams carbohydrate.*

STRAWBERRY SHORTCAKE I

1½ cups flour	½ cup milk
2 teaspoons baking powder	½ teaspoon Sucaryl solution
½ teaspoon salt	1½ quarts strawberries
4 tablespoons shortening	

Sift and mix flour, baking powder, and salt. Work in shortening. Add milk and Sucaryl solution. Roll out to about ¾-inch thickness on floured board. Cut out 6 biscuits and place on greased baking pan. Brush tops of biscuits with milk. Bake at 450 degrees for 12 to 15 minutes. Split biscuits while hot and cover with crushed berries. Serve immediately. 6 servings. *1 serving contains 35 grams carbohydrate.*

STRAWBERRY SHORTCAKE II

SHORTCAKE BISCUIT

1 cup flour	⅓ stick corn oil margarine
¼ teaspoon salt	⅜ cup milk
2 teaspoons baking powder	½ teaspoon liquid sweetener

Sift flour, salt, and baking powder together. Soften margarine but do not melt. Cut into flour mixture with pastry blender or fork to rice sized lumps. Mix sweetener with milk and add to flour mixture to make a fairly soft dough. Knead lightly and turn out on floured breadboard or pastry cloth. Pat and roll to ⅛-inch thickness, cut into 16 3″ rounds. Bake at 425 degrees until light browned. *1 biscuit contains 5 grams carbohydrate.*

STRAWBERRY TOPPING

¼ recipe commercial low
    calorie whipped top-
    ping
¾ cup fresh strawberries

2 saccharin tablets or 1
    package granulated
    sugar substitute

Dissolve sweeteners in 2 tablespoons water. Add few drops red food coloring. 2 tablespoons whipped topping. Carbohydrate does not need to be considered.

APPLE CAKE

1½ cups flour, sifted
 ½ teaspoon salt
  3 teaspoons baking
    powder
  2 tablespoons shortening

¼ cup milk, skim
1 tablespoon Sucaryl
   solution
4 apples, small
1 teaspoon cinnamon

Sift and mix together flour, salt, and baking powder. Cut in shortening. Add milk and Sucaryl solution. Place dough on floured board and roll out to ½″ thickness. Place in shallow greased pan. Pare and slice apples. Press apple slices into dough and sprinkle with cinnamon. Bake for 30 minutes at 350 degrees. Serve with lemon sauce. *1 serving contains 24 grams carbohydrate.*

SPONGE CUP CAKES

  3 eggs, separated
¼ teaspoon salt
¼ teaspoon cream of tartar
  1 teaspoon Sucaryl
    solution

1 teaspoon lemon juice
few gratings lemon rind
½ cup flour, sifted several
   times

Add salt to egg whites and beat until foamy. Add cream of tartar and continue beating until stiff, but not dry. Beat egg yolks until thick. Add Sucaryl solution, lemon juice, and lemon rind while continuing to beat. Quickly and carefully fold egg yolks and flour which has been sifted several times into egg whites. Drop by spoonfuls into greased muffin pans or waxed paper baking cups. Bake for 18 minutes at 350 degrees. 10 cupcakes. *1 cupcake contains 4 grams carbohydrate.*

CHIFFON CAKE

2¼ cups sifted cake flour
3 teaspoons baking powder
1 teaspoon salt
½ cup salad oil
7 eggs, separated
½ cup water

3 tablespoons liquid Sucaryl
2 teaspoons grated lemon rind
1 teaspoon vanilla
½ teaspoon cream of tartar

Preheat oven to 325 degrees. Have eggs at room temperature for best volume when beaten. In small mixer bowl sift together the flour, baking powder, and salt. Make well in center; add oil, egg yolks, water, Sucaryl, lemon rind, and vanilla. Beat until smooth. In large mixer bowl, beat egg whites until foamy; add cream of tartar and beat until very stiff peaks form. Gently fold batter into stiffly beaten egg whites until just blended. (Do not stir.) Turn into an ungreased 9″ tube pan. Bake 65 minutes or until done. Invert cake to cool. 12 servings. *1 serving contains 15 grams carbohydrate.*

ANGEL FOOD CAKE

1 cup and 2 tablespoons cake flour, sifted
½ cup sugar
12 egg whites
1 teaspoon cream of tartar

1 teaspoon vanilla
½ teaspoon almond extract
1 tablespoon Sucaryl solution

Sift flour with sugar and salt 9 times. Beat egg whites until frothy. Add cream of tartar and continue beating until whites will peak but are not dry. Add flavorings and Sucaryl solution. Fold dry ingredients into egg whites as rapidly and carefully as possible. Pour into a large ungreased angel food pan and bake at 325 degrees for one hour until cake shrinks slightly from side of pan. Remove cake from oven and turn upside down to cool. 12 servings. *1 serving contains 15 grams of carbohydrate.*

HAWAIIAN DELIGHT CHEESECAKE

3 tablespoons graham cracker crumbs

2 envelopes (2 tablespoons) unflavored gelatin

½ cup cold water

1 cup unsweetened pineapple chunks, drained (reserve juice)

¾ cup reserved unsweetened pineapple juice or water

1½ cups (12-ounce carton) creamed cottage cheese

3 eggs

¼ teaspoon salt

2 tablespoons unsweetened lemon juice

1 tablespoon liquid sweetener

1 teaspoon vanilla

¼ cup skim milk

1 tablespoon graham cracker crumbs

Sprinkle 3 tablespoons graham cracker crumbs in bottom of 8" or 9" square pan; set aside. Soften gelatin in water. Bring pineapple juice to a boil and stir in softened gelatin. In large mixer bowl, beat cottage cheese at high speed until almost smooth, about 3 minutes. Separate eggs, placing whites in small mixer bowl; yolks in large mixer bowl with cottage cheese. To the cottage cheese blend in salt, lemon juice, liquid sweetener, milk and vanilla; beat well. Blend in dissolved gelatin. Chill, stirring occasionally, until mixture is slightly thickened but not set, about 1 hour. In small mixer bowl, beat egg whites at high speed until soft peaks form; gently fold into gelatin mixture. Carefully pour or spoon over crumbs in pan. Sprinkle remaining 1 tablespoon of crumbs over filling. Top with drained pineapple chunks. Chill until firm, at least 4 hours.

Garnish with fresh strawberries if desired. Makes 9 servings. *1/9 of cake contains 10 grams carbohydrate.*

PASTRY SHELL

1 cup flour	1/3 cup shortening
1/4 teaspoon salt	2 to 3 tablespoons ice water

Sift flour and salt together. Add shortening, cutting it in with a pastry blender or two knives until the mixture has particles of uniform size. Add ice water slowly until dough is rather stiff and will hold together in a ball. Roll out on slightly floured board. Place loosely in an 8″ or 9″ pie pan, leaving 1/2″ extending over the edge of the pan. Build up a fluted edge. Prick the crust with a fork in several places to prevent it from forming blisters. Chill thoroughly in the refrigerator (this may be done while oven is being pre-heated). Bake until a delicate brown at 500 degrees for 8 minutes. 7 servings. *1 serving contains 14 grams carbohydrate.*

NOTE: Orange pastry may be made by adding 2 teaspoons orange rind, grated, and substituting ice cold orange juice for ice water.

GRAHAM CRACKER CRUST I

Graham cracker crumbs	1 teaspoon Sucaryl
(27 crackers)	solution
1/4 cup butter or margarine	

Cream shortening with Sucaryl solution and then add graham crackers gradually, mixing thoroughly. Press crumbs over the bottom and sides of a 9″ pie pan and make a fluting around the edge of the crust. The crust may be baked in a slow oven (temperature 325 degrees: time, 10 minutes) and then chilled before filling, or it may be placed in the refrigerator for several hours and then filled and returned to the refrigerator until ready to serve. 8 servings. *1 serving contains 25 grams carbohydrate.*

GRAHAM CRACKER CRUST II

1 cup graham cracker
   crumbs

2 tablespoons butter,
   melted

Combine crumbs with butter. Press into a 9″ pie pan. Bake at 350 degrees for 8 minutes. Cool thoroughly. *⅛ slice of crust contains 15 grams carbohydrate.*

APPLE PIE

1 unbaked pastry shell
7 or 8 tart apples, sliced
   thin
2 tablespoons flour
½ teaspoon cinnamon
   (or nutmeg)

½ teaspoon salt
2 tablespoons margarine
2 teaspoons Sucaryl
   solution
1 tablespoon lemon
   juice

The unbaked pastry may be used as a lower crust to hold the apples or as a crust to cover them. If it is used as a lower crust, aluminum foil may be used to cover the open pie while baking so that the juices will be retained.

Place sliced apples in pie tin lined with pastry or in a greased pie tin. Blend together flour, cinnamon, and salt mixture with melted margarine. Add Sucaryl solution and lemon juice. Spread over apples. Cover with aluminum foil or pastry. Bake for 45 minutes at 425 degrees. 8 servings. *1 serving contains 23 grams carbohydrate.*

CHERRY PIE

1 unbaked pastry shell
2 cups red cherries, water
   packed
3 tablespoons flour

3 tablespoons cornstarch
1 tablespoon Sucaryl
   solution
¼ cup cherry juice

In preparing pastry shell, make shallow bottom crust, since two cups of cherries will not make the usual thick pie. Any pastry left over may be used as a decorative partial top crust. Place cherries (drained of juice) in pastry shell. Mix flour and cornstarch. Add Sucaryl solution and enough juice to make a thick paste (not thin enough to soak into pastry). Pour over cherries. Cover top with aluminum foil, to prevent open pie from drying out. Bake for 45 minutes at 425 degrees. 7 servings. *1 serving contains 26 grams carbohydrate.*

PINEAPPLE CHEESE PIE

1 envelope gelatin	2 tablespoons lemon juice
¼ cup water	
3 eggs, separated	1 tablespoon Sucaryl solution
1 cup pineapple, crushed	
1 teaspoon lemon rind, grated	1 cup cottage cheese
	¼ teaspoon salt

Soften gelatin in water, 5 minutes. Beat egg yolks slightly in top of double boiler. Add pineapple, lemon rind, lemon juice, and Sucaryl solution. Cook over hot water until thick, stirring constantly. Add gelatin and stir until dissolved. Remove from flame and add cottage cheese which has been mashed to relieve the lumpiness. Cool. When mixture begins to thicken, fold in beaten egg whites and salt. If diet will allow, heap into a graham cracker crust. Chill until set. 8 servings. *1 serving of filling contains 4 grams carbohydrate.*

NOTE: For a variation, one-half cup evaporated milk, whipped, may be substituted for cottage cheese, folding it into the cooled mixture just before folding in egg whites.

CUSTARD PIE

1 chilled unbaked pastry shell	2 teaspoons Sucaryl solution
3 cups milk, skim	½ teaspoon salt
	1½ teaspoons vanilla
3 eggs	¼ teaspoon nutmeg

Scald milk. Beat eggs slightly. Add Sucaryl solution, salt, vanilla, nutmeg, and scalded milk. Pour into chilled unbaked pastry shell and bake at 450 degrees for 10 minutes and then 325 degrees for 30 minutes. 6 servings. *1 serving contains 22 grams carbohydrate.*

FROZEN CHOCOLATE PIE

½ tablespoon cornstarch
2 tablespoons cocoa
⅛ teaspoon salt
½ cup milk, skim, scalded
1 egg, separated

1 teaspoon Sucaryl solution
½ cup evaporated milk
1 teaspoon vanilla
12 graham crackers rolled into crumbs

Mix cornstarch, cocoa, and salt together and blend in scalded milk. Add slightly beaten egg yolk and Sucaryl solution. Cook in top of double boiler until thick. Cool. Fold in beaten evaporated milk and stiffly-beaten egg white. Add vanilla. Place half graham cracker crumbs on bottom of refrigerator tray. Cover with custard and top with remaining crumbs. Freeze until firm. 6 servings. *1 serving contains 20 grams carbohydrate.*

LEMON CHIFFON PIE

9″ graham cracker crust
1 envelope (1 tablespoon) unflavored gelatin
½ cup cold water
3 eggs
3 tablespoons sugar
1 tablespoon liquid sweetener
½ teaspoon grated fresh lemon peel, or ¾ teaspoon lemon extract

⅛ teaspoon salt
¼ cup unsweetened lemon juice
2 to 3 drops yellow food coloring, if desired
⅓ cup instant non-fat dry milk
⅓ cup ice water
1 tablespoon unsweetened lemon juice

Prepare graham cracker crust. In small saucepan, soften gelatin in cold water. Separate eggs, placing whites in small mixer bowl, yolks in saucepan with softened gelatin. To the egg yolks, add sugar, artificial sweetener, lemon peel, salt, lemon juice, and food coloring; blend well. Cook over medium heat, stirring constantly, until mixture just comes to a boil. Remove from heat; cool until slightly thickened. In small mixer bowl, beat reserved egg whites, non-fat dry milk, food coloring, ice water, and lemon juice at high speed until stiff peaks form. By hand, fold gelatin mixture into egg white mixture until well blended. Carefully spoon filling into prepared graham cracker crust. Chill until set, about 2 hours. Makes 8 servings. *⅛ slice of pie contains 21 grams carbohydrate.*

TIP: Place a few ice cubes in water; this is essential for proper whipping.

MOCHA CHIFFON PIE

9″ graham cracker crust
2 envelopes low calorie chocolate pudding
2 cups milk
1 cup hot water
1 rounded teaspoon instant coffee

2 sweetener tablets or 1 package granulated sugar substitute
1 teaspoon unflavored gelatin
2 egg whites beaten to stiff peaks

Mix 2 envelopes with ¼ cup milk until smooth. Then add to 1¾ cups milk. Mix instant coffee and artificial sweetener with 1 cup hot water. Soften unflavored gelatin in a little cold water. Then stir in hot coffee until thoroughly dissolved. Add coffee mixture to pudding mixture. Place over medium heat and cook until it just comes to a boil. Remove from heat and cool, stirring occasionally. When cool, stir smooth, then fold in stiffly beaten egg whites. Pile into graham cracker crust. Chill until set. (NOTE: Use granulated sugar substitute for beating egg whites.) *⅛ pie contains 21 grams carbohydrate.*

PUMPKIN PARFAIT PIE

9″ graham cracker crust
1 envelope (1 tablespoon unflavored gelatin
1½ cups skim milk
1 cup canned or cooked pumpkin
½ teaspoon cinnamon
¼ teaspoon nutmeg
⅛ teaspoon cloves

1 cup vanilla ice cream, softened
2 teaspoons liquid sweetener
½ teaspoon vanilla
3 drops red food coloring
2 drops yellow food coloring

Prepare graham cracker crust. In medium saucepan, soften gelatin in skim milk. Blend in pumpkin and spices. Cook over low heat, stirring constantly, just until mixture comes to a boil; remove from heat. Blend in remaining ingredients until well combined. Chill until slightly thickened but not set. By hand, stir briskly until smooth and pour into prepared crust. Chill until firm, about 2 to 3 hours. ⅛ pie contains 21 grams carbohydrate.

SPINACH SOUFFLÉ PIE

1 9″ unbaked pastry shell
1 egg yolk, slightly beaten
2 cups soft bread crumbs (3 slices)
½ cup whole milk
1 tablespoon grated Parmesan cheese
¼ teaspoon salt

dash ground nutmeg
¼ cup chopped onion
2 tablespoons butter or margarine
2 12-ounce packages frozen spinach
1 egg white, beaten stiffly

Partially bake pastry shell in 450 degree oven for 5 minutes; remove and cool. In large bowl, combine egg yolk, soft bread crumbs, milk, cheese, salt, and nutmeg. Cook onion in butter till tender; add with spinach soufflé to bread mixture. Fold in egg whites. Turn into pie shell.

Bake in 375 degree oven for 45 to 50 minutes. Remove
and cool. Garnish with lemon wedges. 6 servings. *1 serving
contains 25 grams carbohydrate.*

CHOCOLATE CHIP COOKIES I

1 cup sifted flour	½ teaspoon vanilla
½ teaspoon baking soda	1 egg, beaten
¼ teaspoon salt	½ cup semi-sweet
½ cup butter	chocolate pieces
4 teaspoons liquid Sucaryl	(3 ounces)

Preheat oven to 375 degrees. Sift together the dry ingredients. Cream butter; add Sucaryl, vanilla, and egg,
blending well. Add flour mixture and beat well. Stir in the
chocolate pieces. Drop by level teaspoonfuls onto a lightly
greased baking sheet. Bake 8 to 10 minutes. 36 cookies.
4 cookies contain 15 grams carbohydrate.

CHOCOLATE CHIP COOKIES II

⅔ cup shortening	1½ cups flour
⅓ cup sugar	½ teaspoon soda
⅓ cup brown sugar	½ teaspoon salt
1 egg	1 cup semi-sweet
1 teaspoon vanilla	chocolate pieces

Cream together shortening and sugars. Add egg and
vanilla, mixing well. Sift together dry ingredients and add
to creamed mixture. Stir in chocolate chips. Drop by
rounded teaspoons 2 inches apart onto ungreased cookie
sheets. Bake at 375 degrees for 8 to 10 minutes. Makes 4
dozen. *1 cookie contains 10 grams carbohydrate.*

PEANUT BUTTER COOKIES I

¼ cup butter
½ cup peanut butter
2 tablespoons liquid
Sucaryl
⅓ cup skim milk

1 egg
1 teaspoon vanilla
1 cup sifted flour
1 teaspoon baking powder
¼ teaspoon salt

Preheat oven to 375 degrees. Combine butter, peanut butter, and Sucaryl; blend well. Add milk combined with egg and vanilla. Sift, flour, baking powder, and salt together, and add, blending well. Drop by rounded teaspoonfuls onto greased cookie sheet. Flatten with a fork dipped in water. Bake about 10 minutes. 48 cookies. *2 cookies contain 5 grams carbohydrate.*

PEANUT BUTTER COOKIES II

1¼ cups all purpose
flour
½ cup creamy peanut
butter
¼ cup cooking oil
¼ cup water

1 tablespoon liquid
sweetener
1½ teaspoons baking
powder
1 teaspoon vanilla
1 egg

Preheat oven to 375 degrees. In large mixing bowl, combine all ingredients; mix well. Shape into 1 inch balls, using about 1 teaspoon of dough for each. Place 2 inches apart onto ungreased cookie sheets; flatten with fork. Bake at 375 degrees for 12 to 15 minutes or until lightly brown. Store in refrigerator. Makes 42 cookies. *2 cookies contain 7 grams carbohydrate.*

COCONUT SURPRISE COOKIES

1⅓ cups all-purpose flour	½ teaspoon salt
⅔ cup coconut	½ teaspoon baking soda
⅓ cup margarine, softened	1 tablespoon liquid sweetener
¼ cup firmly packed brown sugar	2 teaspoons vanilla
	2 eggs

Preheat oven to 375 degrees. Lightly grease cookie sheets. In large mixing bowl, combine all ingredients; mix well. Drop by teaspoon, 2 inches apart, onto lightly greased cookie sheets. Bake at 375 degrees for 8 to 10 minutes until edges are golden brown. Store in refrigerator. Makes 36 cookies. *2 cookies contain 10 grams carbohydrate.*

OATMEAL COOKIES I

½ cup margarine, softened	1 teaspoon cinnamon
4 teaspoons liquid sweetener	½ teaspoon salt
1 teaspoon vanilla	½ teaspoon baking soda
1 egg	¾ cup cold water
1 cup all-purpose flour	1 cup quick cooking rolled oats
	½ cup raisins, if desired

Preheat oven to 375 degrees. In large mixer bowl, combine margarine, liquid sweetener, vanilla, and egg. Beat 2 minutes at high speed, scraping bowl occasionally, until well blended. Add flour, cinnamon, salt, soda, and water. Beat at low speed until well combined, about 2 minutes. Stir in rolled oats and raisins. (Dough will be soft). Drop by teaspoons, 2 inches apart, onto ungreased cookie sheets. Bake at 375 degrees for 12 to 15 minutes until cookies are set. Store in refrigerator. Makes 42 cookies. *2 cookies contain 10 grams carbohydrate.*

OATMEAL COOKIES II

½ cup margarine	⅛ teaspoon baking soda
1 egg	1 teaspoon cinnamon
1 teaspoon Sucaryl solution	½ teaspoon nutmeg
	¼ teaspoon salt
¼ cup milk	1 teaspoon vanilla
1 cup flour, sifted	½ cup raisins
½ teaspoon baking powder	1 cup rolled oats

Cream margarine. Add beaten egg, Sucaryl solution, and milk. Sift and mix dry ingredients, and then add to first mixture. Beat in vanilla, raisins, and rolled oats. Drop by teaspoon onto greased cookie sheet and bake at 375 degrees for 15 minutes. 30 cookies. *2 cookies contain 14 grams carbohydrate.*

RAISIN COOKIES OR CAKES

1 cup seedless raisins, chopped very fine in food chopper	1 teaspoon baking soda
	2 tablespoons margarine, melted
½ cup cold water	2 teaspoons Sucaryl solution
1½ cups flour, sifted	salt

Combine raisins and water. Mix and sift together flour, soda, and salt. Add to raisin mixture. Add shortening and Sucaryl solution. For cookies: drop by teaspoon onto a greased cookie sheet. For little cakes: pour into greased muffin pans. Bake at 350 degrees for cookies 15 minutes; for cakes 35 minutes. The cakes may be served as pudding, covered with a serving of soft custard. 24 cookies or 12 cakes. *1 cookie contains 10 grams carbohydrate. 1 cake with custard contains 20 grams carbohydrate.*

CHOCOLATE-NUT BROWNIES

1 square unsweetened chocolate	2 eggs, beaten
⅓ cup butter	1 cup sifted cake flour
2 tablespoons Sucaryl solution	½ teaspoon salt
2 teaspoons vanilla	½ teaspoon baking soda
	¾ cup chopped walnuts

Melt the unsweetened chocolate and butter in a sauce-pan over low heat. Remove from heat. Add Sucaryl, vanilla, and the beaten eggs. Stir until well blended. Add sifted cake flour, salt, and baking soda. Mix until blended. Stir in the chopped walnuts. Pour into a greased 8" square pan. Level batter in pan. Bake in a slow oven (325 degrees) for 20 minutes. Cool. Cut into bars. 16 2-inch by 2-inch squares. *1 square contains 8 grams carbohydrate.*

APPLESAUCE COOKIES

1⅔ cups sifted flour	2 tablespoons liquid Sucaryl
½ teaspoon salt	1 egg
1 teaspoon cinnamon	1 cup unsweetened applesauce
½ teaspoon nutmeg	⅓ cup raisins
½ teaspoon cloves	1 cup whole bran cereal
1 teaspoon baking soda	
½ cup butter	

Preheat oven to 375 degrees. Sift together the flour, salt, cinnamon, nutmeg, cloves, and baking soda. Mix butter, Sucaryl, and egg until light and fluffy. Then add flour mixture and applesauce alternately, mixing well after each addition. Fold in raisins and cereal. Drop by level tablespoonfuls onto greased cookie sheet, about 1 inch apart. Bake 18 minutes, or until golden brown. 48 cookies. *1 cookie contains 5 grams carbohydrate.*

PECAN WAFERS

¼ cup margarine or
   butter
¼ teaspoon Sucaryl
   solution

½ cup flour, sifted
½ cup pecans, broken in
   very small pieces
½ teaspoon vanilla

Mix all ingredients together with fingers. Shape into
small balls and then flatten out to wafer size, 1¼″ in di-
ameter. Place on greased cookie sheet and bake at 300
degrees for 45 minutes. 20 cookies. *1 cookie contains 2
grams carbohydrate.*

ORANGE PECAN COOKIES

¼ cup shortening
1 egg
2 teaspoons Sucaryl
   solution
6 tablespoons frozen
   orange juice concen-
   trate (unsweetened)

2 tablespoons water
1 cup flour, sifted
¼ teaspoon baking
   powder
¼ teaspoon salt
1 teaspoon vanilla
¼ cup pecans

Cream shortening and add egg, Sucaryl solution, and
frozen orange concentrate diluted with water. Beat well.
Mix and sift together flour, baking powder, and salt. Add
dry ingredients to first mixture; add vanilla and chopped
pecans. Drop by spoonfuls onto greased baking sheet.
Bake at 375 degrees for 12 to 15 minutes. 30 cookies.
1 cookie contains 4 grams carbohydrate.

Breads

FRENCH TOAST

1 egg
2 tablespoons milk
1 slice bread

2 teaspoons butter or
    margarine

Beat egg until thick and add milk. Dip bread in egg-milk mixture and brown in melted butter in frying pan. *1 serving contains 15 grams carbohydrate.*

CINNAMON TOAST

1 slice bread
1 teaspoon butter or
    margarine

¼ teaspoon cinnamon
¼ teaspoon saccharin
    sweetener powder

Toast bread. Spread with softened margarine. Sprinkle with cinnamon and saccahrine sweetener powder which have been mixed together. *1 serving contains 15 grams carbohydrate*.

WAFFLES

1 cup flour	2 eggs, separated
3 teaspoons baking powder	1 cup milk
½ teaspoon salt	3 teaspoons melted margarine

Sift flour, baking powder, and salt together. Add milk to the beaten egg yolks. Add the egg-milk mixture to the dry ingredients and beat until smooth. Add melted margarine and fold in stiffly-beaten egg whites. Bake in waffle iron. Serve with sugarless waffle syrup or sauce. 8 waffles. *1 waffle contains 14 grams carbohydrate.*

PANCAKES

1 cup flour	1 egg
2 teaspoons baking powder	1 cup milk
¼ teaspoon salt	1 tablespoon melted margarine

Mix and sift dry ingredients; beat egg, add milk, and pour slowly over the first mixture. Beat thoroughly and add melted margarine. Drop by spoonfuls on a hot griddle (greased, if necessary). When pancakes are puffed and full of bubbles turn and cook on other side. Serve with sugarless syrup. 7 large or 14 small cakes. *1 large or 2 small cakes contain 15 grams carbohydrate.*

FAVORITE PANCAKES

1¼ cups flour	½ teaspoon salt
2 teaspoons baking powder	1 beaten egg
½ teaspoon soda	1 cup buttermilk
	2 tablespoons salad oil

Blend egg, milk, and oil. Measure flour after sifting. Blend dry ingredients together. Add to liquids; beat with rotary beater until all flour is moistened. Grease heated griddle if necessary. Pour batter from pitcher or tip of large spoon in pools slightly apart. Turn pancakes as soon as they are puffed and full of bubbles, but before bubbles break. Turn and brown on other side. Serve immediately with butter or margarine. Serve with blueberry sauce or low calorie syrup. Makes 10 4-inch pancakes. *1 4-inch pancake contains 15 grams carbohydrate.*

BAKING POWDER BISCUITS

2 cups flour	1 teaspoon salt
3 teaspoons baking powder	4 tablespoons shortening
	¾ cup milk

Sift flour, baking powder, and salt together. Cut in shortening until it is evenly mixed with dry ingredients. Add milk, mixing well. Knead for ½ minute and roll out to about ½″ thickness. Cut with biscuit cutter. Place on greased baking sheet about 1½ inches apart. Brush with milk and bake at 450 degrees for 12 to 15 minutes. 15 biscuits. *1 biscuit contains 13 grams carbohydrate.* If Bisquick is used, the two cup recipe on the box will make 12 biscuits, the value of each will be the same, 13 grams carbohydrate. Variety can be enjoyed by adding grated cheese or parsley to the mixture.

MUFFINS

1 cup flour, sifted	½ cup milk
1½ teaspoons baking powder	2½ tablespoons melted shortening
½ teaspoon salt	½ teaspoon granulated sugar substitute
1 egg	

Heat oven to 400 degrees. Line muffin cups with paper baking cups. Beat egg with fork. Stir in milk and shortening. Sift flour; blend in dry ingredients; stir just until flour is moistened. Batter should be lumpy. Do not over mix. Fill muffin cups ⅔ full. Bake 20 to 25 minutes or until golden brown. Makes 8 muffins. *1 muffin contains 15 grams carbohydrate.*

CHERRY MUFFINS

6 ounces or ¾ cup biscuit mix
½ cup sugar
¾ cup whole milk
2 tablespoons margarine

1 egg
½ cup cottage cheese
1 cup tart cherries, water packed

Blend milk, margarine, and egg. Stir into combined dry ingredients. Fold in cherries and cottage cheese. Spoon into 12 medium-sized greased muffin tins. Filling ⅔ full. Bake 425 degrees for 20 to 25 minutes. *1 muffin contains 16 grams carbohydrate.*

BLUEBERRY MUFFINS

1½ cups flour, sifted
3 teaspoons baking powder
½ teaspoon salt
1 egg, well-beaten
½ cup milk

1 teaspoon Sucaryl solution
3 teaspoons margarine, melted
⅔ cup blueberries, fresh or well drained canned berries

Mix together sifted flour, baking powder and salt. Add well beaten egg, milk and Sucaryl solution. When partly blended, add melted margarine. Fold in berries. Pour into greased muffin pans and bake at 400 degrees for 25 minutes. 12 muffins. *1 muffin contains 12 grams carbohydrate.*

CORN MEAL MUFFINS

½ cup cornmeal
1 cup flour, sifted
3 teaspoons baking
   powder
½ teaspoon salt
¾ cup milk

1 egg, beaten
1 tablespoon margarine,
   melted
⅜ teaspoon Sucaryl
   solution

Mix and sift dry ingredients. Add milk with beaten egg, melted margarine, and Sucaryl solution gradually. Bake in greased muffin pans at 400 degrees for 25 minutes. 12 muffins. *1 muffin contains 13 grams carbohydrate.*

POPOVERS

2 eggs
1 cup milk
1 cup flour

¼ teaspoon salt
1 tablespoon butter or
   margarine

Beat eggs and add milk while still beating. Then slowly add flour and salt which have been sifted together, continuing to beat in order to prevent lumps. Add melted margarine and pour into hot greased popover pans. Bake 450 degrees 25 minutes then 350 degrees for 15 minutes. 8 popovers. *1 popover contains 14 grams carbohydrate.*

BANANA BREAD

1 pound ripe bananas
   (3 or 4) mashed
1½ packets granulated
   sugar substitute
2 eggs, well beaten

1¼ cups cake flour
3 teaspoons baking
   powder
¼ teaspoon salt

Sprinkle sugar substitute over bananas and stir until dissolved; blend in eggs. Sift together flour, baking powder, and salt. Blend thoroughly into banana mixture but do not overmix. Preheat oven to 350 degrees. Pour batter into greased loaf pan (4″ x 7″). Bake 25 minutes. Reduce heat to 300 degrees and continue baking until done, 35 to 40 minutes. 14 slices. *1 slice contains 15 grams carbohydrate.*

BANANA TEA BREAD

1¾ cups sifted flour
2 teaspoons baking powder
¼ teaspoon baking soda
½ teaspoon salt
¼ cup melted shortening

2 eggs, well beaten
2 tablespoons liquid Sucaryl
1 teaspoon vanilla
2 medium bananas, mashed

Preheat oven to 350 degrees. Sift flour, baking powder, baking soda, and salt together. Combine shortening, eggs, Sucaryl and vanilla. Add to flour mixture stirring only until flour is moistened. Fold in mashed bananas. Turn into a well greased loaf pan (7½″ x 3¾″ x 2½″). Bake 60 minutes or until done. 12 slices. *1 slice contains 16 grams carbohydrate.*

PECAN LOAF

2 cups flour
4 teaspoons baking powder
1 teaspoon salt
3 tablespoons margarine
2 tablespoons butter or other shortening

1 egg, plus 1 egg yolk
1 cup skim milk
½ cup pecans, broken meats

Mix and sift flour, baking powder, and salt. Cut in margarine and other shortening. Add beaten egg, egg yolk, and milk and finally pecans. Sucaryl solution may be added as desired, if a sweeter bread is preferred (2 teaspoons). Turn into a buttered 10″ loaf pan. Let stand 20 minutes and then bake in 350 degree oven for 50 minutes. 20 slices. *1 slice contains 11 grams carbohydrate.*

SPICED FRUIT BREAD

3 cups flour, sifted	1⅓ cups raisins
4½ teaspoons baking powder	2 eggs, beaten
1½ teaspoons salt	1 cup milk
1 teaspoon mace	1 tablespoon Sucaryl solution
½ teaspoon cloves, powdered	4 tablespoons shortening, melted
½ teaspoon nutmeg	

Sift together flour, baking powder, salt, mace, cloves, nutmeg. Stir in raisins. Combine eggs, milk, Sucaryl solution, and shortening, and add to flour mixture. Turn into greased loaf pan, 9" x 5" x 3" and bake at 350 degrees for 1¼ hours. 20 slices. *1 slice contains 21 grams carbohydrate.*

ORANGE DATE BREAD

¼ cup margarine	2 cups flour, sifted
2 eggs, beaten	1 teaspoon baking powder
½ cup, scant, orange juice	½ teaspoon baking soda
½ cup water	½ teaspoon salt
2 teaspoons Sucaryl solution	¼ cup pecans, broken
	10 dates, cut in pieces

Cream margarine and add eggs, orange juice, water, and Sucaryl solution. Add remaining ingredients, beating thoroughly. Pour into greased loaf pan and let stand for 20 minutes before baking. Bake at 350 degrees for 55 minutes. 18 slices. *1 slice contains 13 grams carbohydrate.*

CASSEROLE RAISIN BREAD

2 cups biscuit mix	½ cup raisins
⅓ cup quick-cooking oatmeal	1 egg, well beaten
1 teaspoon baking powder	1¼ cups skim milk
¼ teaspoon salt	4½ teaspoons liquid Sucaryl

Preheat oven to 350 degrees. Combine mix, oatmeal, baking powder, salt, and raisins. Combine remaining ingredients; add to dry ingredients all at once. Blend well, pour into a lightly greased 1-quart round casserole. Bake 50 to 60 minutes or until done. Cool in casserole 10 minutes before turning out on wire rack. 16 servings. *1 serving contains 16 grams carbohydrate.*

CINNAMON COFFEE CAKE

TOPPING

1 tablespoon melted margarine or butter	½ teaspoon liquid Sucaryl
½ teaspoon cinnamon	¼ cup toasted dry bread crumbs

CAKE

2 cups sifted cake flour	¾ cup skim milk
3 teaspoons baking powder	1 tablespoon liquid Sucaryl
¼ teaspoon salt	4 drops yellow food coloring
3 tablespoons soft margarine	1 egg

Preheat oven to 375 degrees. Grease an 8″ round cake pan. Combine topping ingredients, stirring until blended; set aside: Sift flour, baking powder, and salt into small mixer bowl. Cut in margarine on low, then medium, speed, 3 to 5 minutes, until mixture is completely blended and looks like fine corn meal. Add ½ cup of the milk mixed with Sucaryl and coloring. Beat ½ minute on medium speed. Add remaining milk and beat one minute longer. Add unbeaten egg and beat one minute more. Pour into prepared pan; sprinkle with cinnamon crumbs. Bake 20 minutes or until cake springs back when lightly touched. 8 servings. *1 serving contains 23 grams carbohydrate.*

ORANGE-MARMALADE NUT BREAD

2 cups sifted flour
1½ teaspoons baking powder
½ teaspoon baking soda
¼ teaspoon salt
⅓ cup skim milk
1 egg
2 tablespoons melted butter
1 tablespoon Sucaryl solution
½ cup dietetic orange marmalade
½ cup chopped walnuts

Combine flour, baking powder, soda, and salt in mixing bowl. Combine skim milk, egg, butter, Sucaryl; add to flour mixture mixing only until flour is dampened. Fold in marmalade and nuts, mixing as little as possible. Spoon batter into lightly greased 9″ x 5″ x 3″ loaf pan. Bake in moderate oven, 350 degrees for 1 hour and 40 minutes. Cool before slicing. 12 slices. *1 slice contains 15 grams carbohydrate.*

PRIZE WINNING OZARK PUMPKIN BREAD

1⅔ cups sifted flour
1 teaspoon baking soda
⅛ teaspoon salt
½ teaspoon cinnamon
½ teaspoon nutmeg
⅓ cup shortening
1⅓ cups sugar
2 eggs
1 cup mashed canned pumpkin
⅓ cup cooking sherry or domestic sherry
½ cup chopped pecans
¼ teaspoon baking powder

Grease a 9" x 5" loaf pan. Sift together flour, baking powder, soda, salt, cinnamon, and nutmeg. Cream together shortening and sugar. Add eggs one at a time and beat well after each addition. Stir in mashed pumpkin. Add dry ingredients alternately with sherry and blend well after each additional. Fold in nuts. Bake at 350 degrees for 1 hour or until brown. Cool thoroughly. 18 slices. *1 slice contains 24 grams carbohydrate.*

Alcoholic Beverages

Carbohydrate Content of Some of the Alcoholic Beverages

Type	Amount	Carbohydrate Grams
Ale, mild	8 ounces	8
Beer	12 ounces	16
Gin, rum, vodka, whiskey	1½ ounces	0
Brandy, California	1 brandy glass	0
Anisette	1 cordial glass	7
Brandy, apricot	1 cordial glass	6
Benedictine	1 cordial glass	7
Crème de Menthe	1 cordial glass	6
Curaco	1 cordial glass	6
Gin rickey	1 glass	0
Daiquiri	1 cocktail glass	5
Manhattan	3½ ounces	8
Martini	3½ ounces	0
Old-Fashioned	4 ounces	4
Planter's punch	1 glass	8
Tom collins	10 ounces	9
Domestic champagne	4 ounces	3
Muscatelle or port	3½ ounces	14
Sauterne, California	3½ ounces	4
Domestic sherry	2 ounces	5
French vermouth, dry	3½ ounces	0
Italian, vermouth, sweet	3½ ounces	12

NOTE: 1 brandy glass = 30 cc.   1 Burgundy glass = 120 cc.
       1 cordial glass = 20 cc.   1 Champagne glass = 150 cc.
       1 cocktail glass = 90 cc.

Miscellaneous

Carbohydrate Content of Some Sweets

Sweets	Carbohydrate Grams
8 apricot halves stuffed with cream cheese and topped with nuts	22
8 dates stuffed with cream cheese	41
8 prunes stuffed with cream cheese-orange concentrate combination	46
8 cream cheese-orange concentrate balls rolled in pecans	7
8 cream cheese with orange rind balls rolled in coconut	12
8 cream cheese-orange concentrate balls dipped in melted chocolate and dropped on waxed paper	22
8 chocolate wafers—melted—chocolate flavored with few drops of peppermint or vanilla extract and dropped by teaspoon on waxed paper	16
8 chocolate raisin clusters—5 or 6 raisins dipped in melted chocolate and dropped from spoon onto waxed paper	26
8 chocolate coconut dips—coconut dipped in melted chocolate and dropped from spoon on waxed paper	27
8 cream cheese, orange rind and raisins	11

Amount of food for the above recipes

- 8 apricot halves
- 8 dates
- 8 prunes
- 2 tablespoons raisins
- 12 pecan nuts finely chopped
- ¼ cup coconut toasted
- ½ package cream cheese
- 1 tablespoon frozen orange concentrate
- 1 teaspoon orange rind and 1 teaspoon Sucaryl solution
- 2 squares chocolate, unsweetened, melted, and crushed

COCOA SQUARES

1 envelope gelatin	½ teaspoon Sucaryl solution
¼ cup water	
2½ teaspoons cocoa	2 tablespoons evaporated milk
2 teaspoons margarine	
⅛ teaspoon salt	½ teaspoon vanilla
¼ cup water	⅛ teaspoon cinnamon

Soften gelatin in ¼ cup water, 5 minutes. Mix cocoa and ¼ cup water and heat simmering 5 minutes. Add margarine, salt, Sucaryl solution, and gelatin. Stir until dissolved and remove from fire. Add evaporated milk, vanilla, and cinnamon. Pour into small shallow pan rinsed in cold water. Place in refrigerator to set. Cut in squares. 8 pieces. 1 piece need not be considered for carbohydrate. *3 pieces contain 3 grams carbohydrate.*

CHOCOLATE PECAN FUDGE

1 envelope gelatin	¾ teaspoon Sucaryl solution
¼ cup water	
1 square unsweetened chocolate	¼ cup water
	½ cup evaporated milk
⅛ teaspoon cinnamon	½ teaspoon vanilla extract
	¼ cup pecans, chopped

Soften gelatin in ¼ cup water 5 minutes. Melt chocolate with cinnamon and Sucaryl solution. Add slowly evaporated milk and water. Add gelatin and stir until dissolved. Remove from fire and add vanilla. Cool. When mixture begins to thicken add nuts. Turn into tin rinsed in cold water. When firm, cut into 6 pieces. *1 piece contains 4 grams carbohydrate.*

NUT SPREAD

½ cup unroasted cashews
¼ cup sesame seeds
¼ cup shelled sunflower
      seeds

3 tablespoons salad oil
¼ teaspoon salt
⅓ cup chopped raisins
      (optional)

In blender container, combine the cashews, sesame seeds, and sunflower seeds. Cover and blend on low speed till finely chopped; then on medium-high speed till pureed smooth. (If crunchier butter is preferred, blend at medium-high speed only till desired degree of smoothness is reached.) Stop often and scrape puree from side of container. Add oil and salt and blend till smooth. Carbohydrate does not need to be considered. (*If the raisins are added then 1 tablespoon of the spread is 8 grams carbohydrate.*) ⅔ cup.

SNACK

¾ cup Kix dry cereal
dash salt
dash dry mustard

2 teaspoons margarine or
      butter
2 teaspoons of Parmesan
      cheese

Mix thoroughly. *1 serving contains 15 grams carbohydrate.*

APPLE JELLY

2 teaspoons unflavored
    gelatin
2 cups unsweetened apple
    juice
2 tablespoons liquid
    sweetener

1½ tablespoons lemon
    juice
yellow food coloring, if
    desired

Soften gelatin in ½ cup of the apple juice. Bring remaining 1½ cups juice to a boil; remove from heat. Add softened gelatin, stirring to dissolve. Add liquid sweetener, lemon juice, food coloring. Bring to a rolling boil. Ladle into clean half-pint jars; seal. Keep in refrigerator. Makes 2 half-pint jars. 1 tablespoon does not need to be considered for carbohydrate. *2 tablespoons contain 5 grams carbohydrate.*

GRAPE JELLY

2 teaspoons unflavored
    gelatin
½ cup water

1½ cups unsweetened
    grape juice
2 tablespoons liquid
    sweetener (artificial)

Soften gelatin in water. Bring grape juice to a boil; remove from heat. Add softened gelatin, stirring to dissolve. Add liquid sweetener. Bring to a rolling boil. Ladle into clean half-pint jars; seal. Keep in refrigerator. Makes 2 half-pint jars. 1 tablespoon does not need to be considered for carbohydrate. *2 tablespoons contain 5 grams carbohydrate.*

REFRIGERATOR STRAWBERRY JAM

1½ teaspoons unflavored
    gelatin
1½ tablespoons cold water
3 cups strawberries,
    crushed

1½ tablespoons Sucaryl
¼ teaspoon ascorbic acid
    powder
red food coloring, if desired

Soften gelatin in cold water. Combine strawberries and Sucaryl solution in saucepan. Place over high heat and stir constantly until mixture comes to boil. Remove from heat; add softened gelatin; return to heat and continue to cook for 1 minute. Remove from heat; blend in ascorbic acid powder and food coloring. Ladle into clean half-pint jars; seal. Store in refrigerator. Makes 2 half-pint jars. If no more than 1 tablespoon is used, need not consider the carbohydrate. *4 tablespoons contain 5 grams carbohydrate.*

SUGAR-FREE APPLE JELLY

4 teaspoons unflavored
  gelatin
2 cups unsweetened apple
  juice
2 tablespoons liquid
  Sucaryl

1½ tablespoons lemon
  juice
yellow food coloring if
  desired

Soften gelatin in ½ cup of the apple juice. Bring to boil the remaining 1½ cups juice; remove from heat. Add softened gelatin, stirring to dissolve. Add Sucaryl, lemon juice, and food coloring. Bring to full rolling boil. Ladle into clean half-pint jars; seal. Keep in refrigerator. Makes 2 half-pint jars. *2 tablespoons contain 5 grams carbohydrate.*

Questions and Answers

Q. Can you use any sugar substitute in cooking or heating?

A. Not all are suitable. Saccharin is not good after prolonged heating.

Q. What about sorbitol and mannitol?

A. These are slower absorbing sugars. It is best to avoid these as they are counted as carbohydrate and difficult to work into the meal plan.

Q. Because cheese is a by-product of milk is it avoided in the diet?

A. There is no restriction on the usage of cheese in the diet. The carbohydrate lactose or milk sugar in milk is converted to lactic acid during the cheese making process. Cheese is a very good source of protein.

Q. What about the low-calorie beverages on the market?

A. Read the label to note if sugar is used in small

amounts. Some of the low-calorie beverages contain a small amount of sugar. Avoid these.

Q. Why is it important to spread the carbohydrate throughout the day?

A. It is important to keep the blood sugar levels about the same throughout the day.

Q. What is the difference between *hypo-* and *hyper*glycemia?

A. Hypoglycemia refers to a condition in which the blood sugar (glucose) content of the blood is lower than normal. In hyperglycemia, the blood sugar (glucose) content is higher than normal.

Q. What is insulin?

A. It is a chemical produced by the pancreas gland.

Q. What are the symptoms of low blood sugar?

A. The symptoms are shaking, trembling, sweating.

Q. If you are supposed to avoid concentrated sweets as candy, etc. and limit the intake of carbohydrate in your diet, why are you permitted to use sugar when you are experiencing the symptoms of low blood sugar?

A. Because you are experiencing the condition similar to one in which too much insulin is being injected into your system.

Q. What is the difference between Jello and dietetic gelatin?

A. Jello is a commercial trade name containing sugar sweetened gelatin powder. Dietetic gelatin will contain gelatin, flavoring, coloring material and artificial sweetener.

Q. What do you mean by a dietetic food?

A. One that has not had sugar or salt added in the processing.

Q. Some artificial sweeteners contain sodium and some calcium, may either be used?

A. Yes, unless your physician has sodium restricted in your diet. Then use the calcium one.

Q. Are dietetic breakfast cereals allowed?
A. Yes. Puffed and flaked cereals may be sweetened with artificial sweetener. Avoid those sugar coated.

Q. Is it wise to carry something in case of an emergency to meet the condition of low blood sugar?
A. Yes. Anything with concentrated form of sugar can be used. Sugar lumps, hard candies and raisins. Raisins are available in small packages and can be carried in hot weather and are high in fruit sugars.

Q. Why are the protein foods and the fat foods not limited in the diet?
A. Protein and fat do not stimulate the pancreas to release more insulin.

Q. Why are carbohydrates and sugars limited in the diet?
A. Carbohydrates and sugars do stimulate the pancreas to put out more insulin.

Q. Some of the artificial sweeteners contain lactose and dextrin or dextrose, what are these?
A. Lactose is the milk sugar, and dextrin or dextrose is obtained by the hydrolysis of starch. These are to be considered in the overall amount of carbohydrate in the diet. Artificial sweeteners are on the market that do not contain these items and therefore will be more desirable to use.

Q. Is there a low calorie sweetener derived from protein?
A. A new natural sweetener (up to 3,000 times more intense by weight than sugar) has been isolated. The sweetener called "Monellin" is derived from a wild red berry that grows abundantly in tropical West Africa. It is free of carbohydrates, as are cyclamate and saccharin, but, unlike these is a natural protein. As a carbohydrate-free protein, it could have wide usage as a sugar substitute.

References

1. Bowes, H. N., and Church, C. F. *Food Values of Portions Commonly Used*. 10th ed. Philadelphia: J. B. Lippincott, 1966.
2. Krause, M. V. *Food, Nutrition and Diet Therapy*. 4th ed. Philadelphia: W. B. Saunders, 1968.
3. Wohl, M. G., and Goodhart, R. S. *Modern Nutrition in Health and Disease*. 4th ed. Philadelphia: Lea & Febiger, 1968.
4. Robinson, C. H. *Normal and Therapeutic Nutrition*. 13th ed. New York: The Macmillan Company, 1967.
5. Pike, R. L., and Brown, M. L. *Nutrition: An Integrated Approach*, New York: John Wiley & Sons, Inc., 1967.
6. *Let's Talk About Food*. Chicago, Department of Foods and Nutrition, American Medical Association, 1967.
7. Watt, B. K., and Merrill, A. L. "Compositions of Foods: Raw, Processed, Prepared." *Agriculture Handbook No. 8*. United States Department of Agriculture, December, 1963.

8. "Nutritive Value of Foods." *Home and Garden Bulletin No. 72.* United States Department of Agriculture, January, 1971.

9. Revell, D. *Gourmet Recipes for Diabetics.* Charles C Thomas, Publishers, 1971.

10. *Fruit Fix-Ups.* The Diabetes Education Center, Minneapolis, Minnesota.

11. *Low Calorie Cooking with Sucaryl.* Abbott Laboratories, North Chicago, Illinois.

Index